EITHER CATHOLICISM OR LIBERALISM

Either Catholicism or Liberalism

THE PASTORAL AND
CIRCULAR LETTERS OF
ST. EZEQUIEL MORENO Y DÍAZ

Translation and Foreword by
BRIAN WELTER

AROUCA
PRESS

CONTENTS

NOTE FROM THE
GERMAN TRANSLATOR

"A BISHOP THAT OUR TIMES NEED"—
these words, spoken by St. Ezequiel Moreno in eulogy
of his friend Pedro Schumacher, the saintly bishop of
Portoviejo in Ecuador, best characterize Msgr. Moreno
himself. The zealous missionary, the exemplary religious,
the intrepid bishop, the generous victim soul: all these
roles St. Ezequiel fulfilled with perfection. He stands
out most for his actions in his fight against Liberalism:
while in our days we are often prone to fighting only its
symptoms, such as abortion, the holy Augustinian bishop
sought to remove the source of many, if not all, of modern
society's ills: the pernicious doctrines of Liberalism. His
enemies called him narrowminded and backwards. But
Bishop Moreno was not influenced by such motives as
personal rigidity. While living on three continents in
diverse settings, he showed great flexibility in adapting
to different conditions. Instead, his thoughts and actions
rooted exclusively in his love of God and neighbor. Having realized that the errors of Liberalism do enormous
dishonor to God and put at peril the societal order of
nations willed by their Creator and the eternal fate of
individuals, he considered it his pastoral duty to continu-
ously warn against these false teachings, not shying away
from naming their main proponents' names. Rather timid
and soft-spoken by nature, he drew all his strength from
the Sacred Heart of Jesus: "Fortitudo mea et refugium
meum es tu"—"thou art my strength and my refuge", as
his episcopal motto read.

As Msgr. Moreno's German translator and biographer,
it is a great joy for me that through the initiative of
Alexandros Barbas and Brian Welter, the writings of St.

Ezequiel Moreno y Díaz are made more widely accessible in the form of an English translation. May his life and writings inspire laypeople, religious, priests and (future) bishops alike.

Landsberg am Lech
Feast of St. Vincent of Paul, 2022
Konstantin Stäbler

Foreword

BRIAN WELTER

Many think it is prudent to acquiesce to the demands of the enemies of Jesus Christ. However, the disastrous results that we have encountered demonstrate this to be prudence of the flesh, which is death. We are surrounded by dangers, and new torments threaten us. The enemies of religion and the country do not cease in their determination to ruin everything. They multiply their attacks, not only on the battlefield, but also in the field of ideas and customs in order to bring erroneous understanding and vice to the heart.

—*St. Ezequiel Moreno y Díaz*

S T. EZEQUIEL MORENO Y DÍAZ WAS born on April 9, 1848 in Alfaro, Spain. Like his older brother Eustachio, he became a friar of the Augustinian Recollects and missionary to the Philippines. His work there lasted from 1870 to 1885. He was summoned to Spain at the age of 35 to be the rector of his order's college in Monteagudo, Navarra. But he was soon called to be a missionary again, this time to Colombia in 1888, where he served for the remainder of his active vocation by organizing the work of his order there. He was consecrated bishop on May 1, 1894 for the newly-created apostolic vicariate of Casanare and appointed bishop of Pasto in the next year. He returned to Spain in 1906 for treatment for cancer of the palate, but died on August 19, 1906 at the age of 58 in Monteagudo. He was beatified by Pope Paul VI on November 1, 1975, and canonized by Pope John Paul II on October 11, 1992. He is the patron saint for cancer patients.

Moreno's writings express admirable steadfastness sustained by confidence in both the Church and Christ. This steadfastness came from deep religious roots. Like many saints, the author of these compelling writings grew up in humble and religious circumstances. From an early age, Moreno y Díaz wanted to be a friar. He was a faithful member of his order. In his writings as a bishop, he repeatedly refers to St. Augustine, his order's patron saint, as his master. He fulfilled the charism of his order, which a contemporary source defines as "an experience of the Holy Spirit which implies a specific way of life, a specific mission and spirituality, a style of fraternal living, and a readiness to serve in the mission of the Church."[1]

St. Ezequiel's faithfulness served him well in his vocation. He spent almost his entire adult life on missions. In the Philippines, he learned Tagalog, was ordained to the priesthood (on June 3, 1871), served as a military chaplain in remote areas, and suffered from malaria. He had lost none of this zeal when, years later, shortly after Pope Leo had appointed Moreno to lead the newly-established vicariate of Casanare, Fray Ezequiel "visited the territory, filled with zeal, riding a mule."[2] In his letters to Colombians, he passionately recalls his time ministering to the poorest in forests and near rivers, and struggling with the fierce elements, simple food, and even caimans. He was not drawn to a life of comfort,

1   https://www.stritascentre.org/augustinian-recollect-order.
2   Eugenio Ayape, *Semblanza de San Ezequiel Moreno* (Madrid: Augustinus, 1994), 38.

xii

as these writings clearly show, but to one of service to the Church and others. His steadfastness was always accompanied with a sense of gratitude that he was able to serve Christ and the people in these missions.

This sense of service matches the contemporary understanding of the vocation of the order. The website of the Augustinian Recollects explains,

> The Order came into being in the 16th century when a group of Augustinian religious, under the impulse of the Holy Spirit, discovered among themselves a collective charism by which they sought to live a life of renewed fervour and of new norms at the service of the Church.
>
> The Chapter of the Province of Castile celebrated in Toledo, Spain, in the year 1588, determined that in certain houses of the province, this new manner of life would be lived. Within a few years of the initiation of the Recollection, in 1605, the number of these religious departed on their first missionary expedition to the Philippines.
>
> The Augustinian Recollects of today are heirs to a form of life first initiated by St. Augustine (354–430) and revised in the 13th century with a mendicant style by the Order of St. Augustine in the Great Union of 1256. After more than three centuries of existence, the Recollects were recognized by the Church as an autonomous religious order.[3]

St. Ezequiel's letters and the testimonies of those who knew him indicate that he succeeded in living out the best of the order's history. The Recollects first arrived in Casanare in 1662, and continued their work there into the early nineteenth century. In 1816, they could count on over one-hundred priests, brothers, and novices.

---

3 https://www.stritascentre.org/augustinian-recollect-order.

Unfortunately, the winds of change coming from revolutionary France did not spare Colombia. Colombians may have hoped for a bright future upon their independence on July 20, 1810. However, the ensuing decades brought terrible challenges to the country's Catholic Church in both the institutional structures in large cities such as Bogota, the capital, and in the missionary lands such as the lightly-populated yet vast Casanare, inhabited mostly by indigenous peoples and the descendants of African slaves. The Church's presence, including its missionary work, was dramatically weakened after the expulsion of the Jesuits in 1767. The number of Catholic missionaries steadily fell in the ensuing decades.

This decline was the outcome of policies that deliberately targeted the Church. Between 1821 and 1832, the liberal government in Bogota suppressed many centers of the Recollects, including at Popa, Panama, Tunja, and Honda.[4] One writer notes the hypocrisy of the liberals: "They proclaimed freedom of education, but denied the freedom to teach religion. They spoke a lot about human rights, but did not respect the rights of Catholics."[5] The advocates of this upheaval, wherever it took place, were inspired by the French Revolution's elevation of man above God and advocacy of reason that operates not only independently of faith, but often actively *against* religious belief.[6]

Colombia's return to a conservative government in 1880 under the leadership of Rafael Núñez, along with a new constitution in 1886, brought some relief from

---

4   P. Ángel Peña, *San Ezequiel Moreno: Un valiente misionero* (Lima, 2013), 20–21.
5   Ibid., 84.
6   Pope Pius IX's *Syllabus of Errors* (1864) condemns the following assertion: "All the truths of religion proceed from the innate strength of human reason; hence reason is the ultimate standard by which man can and ought to arrive at the knowledge of all truths of every kind."

the spiritual war. Perhaps most crucially, the hostility between Church and state was transformed into close cooperation. With Núñez's health in decline, the constitution's author, Miguel Antonio Caro, became the dominant conservative figure and a close collaborator of St. Ezequiel. These years of national regeneration after 1880 gave the Church a key role in rebuilding society after what conservatives saw as years of liberal-led decay.[7] Colombia's leadership turned to the Catholic Church to build much-needed culture, education, and welfare, particularly in the territories where St. Ezequiel worked. In 1888, Colombia's government signed a concordat with the Holy See that granted the Church educational and other social privileges. It was "the most favorable agreement for the Holy See that it negotiated in Latin America."[8]

St. Ezequiel played a prominent role in this difficult foundational work. As in the Philippines, his territories were mostly populated by indigenous peoples who were in need of catechesis. Making things more unstable and challenging, the diocese of Pasto bordered Ecuador for 600 kilometers. Ecuador's capital Quito was much closer to Pasto than Bogota. This proximity became much more significant for St. Ezequiel after the liberal defeat of the conservatives in 1895 in Ecuador. Quito under Eloy Alfaro was as liberal and anti-Catholic as Bogota was conservative and pro-Catholic. Pasto, founded in 1539 and the country's third largest city at the time, was destabilized.[9] Moreno was faced with both Ecuadorian revolutionaries and Catholic refugees crossing the porous

7   Holbein Giraldo Paredes, "San Ezequiel Moreno Díaz: 'El liberalismo es pecado. El catolicismo ultramontano en Colombia," *Critero Libre Jurídico* 16 (2011): 35.
8   Alfonso Rubio Hernandez and Juan David Murillo Sandoval, "Ezequiel Moreno Díaz. Obispo en la regeneración de Colombia: La geopolítica contraliberal, 1896–1905," *Berceo* 162 (2012): 215.
9   Peña, 73.

border. Pasto became "the principal base of operations for conservative Ecuadorians who had fled the triumph of the liberal revolution of 1895."[10]

Unsurprisingly, it was as bishop of Pasto that Moreno was most active in his polemics with the liberals.[11] This was when he published his most well-known work, *O con Jesucristo o contra Jesucristo. O Catolicismo o liberalismo*, in 1898. The book was part of the war of words between the pro- and anti-Church camps. Ecuador-based publications targeted conservative bishops such as Fray Ezequiel and the German-born Lazarist Peter Schumacher, bishop of Portoviejo, Ecuador, who took refuge in Colombia after Ecuador's conservatives lost the battle of Gatazo on August 14, 1895. Later, Ecuador's liberal government openly meddled in Colombia's civil war, which was fought between 1899 and 1902, on the anti-Catholic side.[12] Bishop Ezequiel's vehemence against liberals undoubtedly came in large part from his first-hand experience of revolutionary violence.

In his missionary zeal and struggle against liberalism, which he saw above all as a spiritual war, St. Ezequiel enjoyed the support of the Church. Colombia came to be one of the countries that most energetically followed the Church's conservative program.[13] Nineteenth-century popes did not shy away from challenging anti-traditional, liberal, and freemason thinking which sought to undermine the Church's teaching and position in society. A series of encyclicals made the magisterium's position clear.

---

10   Aléxis Medina, "La contrarrevolución en el exilio: Clérigos y conservadores ecuatorianos en Pasto en los primeros años de la Revolución liberal ecuatoriana, 1895–1902," in *E. I. A. L., Estudios Interdisciplinarios de América Latina y el Caribe* (Tel Aviv University, 2022) 151.

11   Paredes, 34.

12   Peña, 73–74.

13   Hernandez and Sandoval, 204.

Often, both the popes and St. Ezequiel mentioned freemasons in the same breath as liberals. The papal opposition to freemasonry began as early as Pope Clement XII's *In Eminenti* of 1738, in which the dangers to Christian spirituality and the task of the Church as shepherd are highlighted:

> We are taught by the divine word that it is the part of faithful servant and of the master of the Lord's household to watch day and night lest such men as these break into the household like thieves, and like foxes seek to destroy the vineyard; in fact, to prevent the hearts of the simple being perverted, and the innocent secretly wounded by their arrows, and to block that broad road which could be opened to the uncorrected commission of sin and for the other just and reasonable motives known to Us.

St. Ezequiel lived out this call to the "faithful servant" by keeping close watch over the effects of liberalism on the faithful.

In 1864, Pope Pius IX, with his encyclical *Quanta cura*, to which he annexed the *Syllabus errorum*, stridently denounced liberalism and its spiritual effects: "The monstrous portents of opinion which prevail especially in this age, bringing with them the greatest loss of souls and detriment of civil society itself; which are grievously opposed also, not only to the Catholic Church and her salutary doctrine and venerable rights, but also to the eternal natural law engraven by God in all men's hearts, and to right reason; and from which almost all other errors have their origin."[14] Moreno's writings would have a similar emotional appeal decades later, as he too linked these "monstrous portents" to the loss of souls.

The saint's writings would echo *Quanta cura*'s description of the spiritual struggle that encompassed all of

---

14   Pope Pius IX, Encyclical letter *Quanta cura* (1864).

society, from the individual to the corporate entity to the highest levels of government. Pope Pius IX noted:

> But, although we have not omitted often to proscribe and reprobate the chief errors of this kind, yet the cause of the Catholic Church, and the salvation of souls entrusted to us by God, and the welfare of human society itself, altogether demand that we again stir up your pastoral solicitude to exterminate other evil opinions, which spring forth from the said errors as from a fountain. Which false and perverse opinions are on that ground the more to be detested, because they chiefly tend to this, that that salutary influence be impeded and (even) removed, which the Catholic Church, according to the institution and command of her Divine Author, should freely exercise even to the end of the world—not only over private individuals, but over nations, peoples, and their sovereign princes; and (tend also) to take away that mutual fellowship and concord of counsels between Church and State which has ever proved itself propitious and salutary, both for religious and civil interests.[15]

Moreno's repeated quotes from the *Syllabus* reflect his advocacy of this position. His writings cannot be understood without *Quanta cura* and other papal teachings.

These teachings identified the spirit of liberalism manifesting in various ways and places around the world. In 1873 in *Etsi multa*, Pope Pius IX denounced the wars fought against the Church and placed the anti-Catholic movements in the Americas within the larger context of battles that the Church was fighting elsewhere, such as the *Kulturkampf* in Germany or anti-Catholic legislation in Switzerland. Perhaps the pope had Ecuador's government in mind when he wrote, "Nor, truly, are

---

15   Pope Pius IX, *Quanta cura.*

things much better or more peaceful in America, several of whose regions are so hostile to Catholics that their governments seem to deny in deeds their Catholic faith. For there, some years past, a most severe war was begun against the Church, its institutions, and the rights of this Apostolic See."[16] Pope Leo XIII continued this condemnation with the encyclicals *Immortale Dei* (1885), *Libertas* (1888), and *Sapientiae Christianae* (1890). Clearly, the Church's battle with liberalism was not letting up in St. Ezequiel's most active years of leadership.

Just like the popes in Rome, so St. Ezequiel in Colombia did not shy away from controversy, particularly when it came to liberals. His zealous opposition to their movement focused his energies during Colombia's civil war, the Guerra de los Mil Días (War of 1000 Days), which pitted Catholics against liberals, the latter of whom were supported by Ecuador's anti-Catholic government. Ezequiel supported both the Catholic soldiers and their families back home praying for victory. This zeal for the charism of his order, to be open to "an experience of the Holy Spirit," put him at odds with the modern world. The spread of liberalism marked Moreno's entire life. Perhaps it seems appropriate that he was born in the year of European revolution, 1848, when the remnants of the *ancien regime* were once again directly challenged with violence. However, although St. Ezequiel defended some aspects of the *ancien regime*, it would be erroneous to call him a defender of the old order. He did not wish to return to a mythical or romanticized medieval or aristocratic past. Accordingly, he accepted any type of political structure, including republicanism.

Some of St. Ezequiel's opponents accused him of simply being a product of Carlist Spain.[17] Perhaps they hoped that

16   Pope Pius IX, Encyclical letter *Etsi multa* (1873).
17   Carlism arose from a dynastic and cultural dispute in Spain

the Colombians would thereby reject him for apparently seeking a return to Spanish colonization. In fact, such accusations did not seem to weaken the strong support the saint enjoyed from his fellow clergy and the people, who clearly saw him as a living saint, not as someone out to advance his own political career. St. Ezequiel does not express a preference for the Spanish crown or for the aggrandizement of Spain in the New World in any of the writings found in this book. The reader gets the impression that St. Ezequiel worked only for Christ.

What he opposed so ferociously and consistently was a certain spirit. He argued that this liberal spirit could infect any political structure or even operate outside of political structures. In other words, the liberal spirit existed in the thinking and attitudes of people. What he defended was not the old political order, Europe's nobles and royalty, or the rapidly-shrinking Spanish empire. He defended Jesus Christ and the Church. He called for a robust faith and defense of the Church. He sensed that he was in the middle of a great spiritual war, and had been called to defend the souls of the faithful. His foray into politics was done as part of this defense.

What did Moreno-Díaz mean by "liberalism"? His view was shared by Nicolas Casas, an Augustine Recollect serving in Colombia at the time, who warned:

> An enormous error is to believe that there are various types of liberalism: one political and another religious; one European and another

---

in 1830. The movement emphasized the country's traditional Catholic and royalist roots within a Christian civilization. It therefore strongly opposed the French Revolution and its political and cultural influence in the nineteenth century. Carlism's supporters believed that modernism aimed to destroy Christianity. See: Francisco Elias de Tejada y Spínola, Rafael Hambre Ciudad, and Francisco Puy Muñoz, *Que es el Carlismo?* (Madrid: Centro de Estudios Históricos y Políticos, 1971), 25.

American . . . *one and the same* is the constitut-
ing principle of it; it's essence is *the same* in
every part, that is, man's rebellion against God's
authority, directly or indirectly."[18]

Both Casas and St. Ezequiel were strongly convinced
that liberalism aimed to "expel Christ from society, the
family, and the very souls of the faithful. It was, therefore,
a grave and constant danger for the faith of his flock.[19]
Casas, like St. Ezequiel, followed Pope Pius IX in regarding hybrid liberals — those who called themselves Catholic
and liberal at the same time — as the most dangerous sort
of liberal because they hid the true nature of liberalism
and worked among the faithful as if they themselves were
pious. Ecuador's progressives, who tried to strike a middle
road between Catholic ultramontanism and revolutionary
liberalism, and who led the country between 1883 and
1894, strongly impacted neighboring Pasto.[20]

Moreno-Díaz was at heart a shepherd. This series of
writings is a pastoral theology. Its author addresses the
spiritual, philosophical, social, and political problems
that he sees his people struggling with. He offers them
the teachings and sacraments of the Church as a solution. Perhaps as a witness to the effects of liberalism,
Moreno does not shy away from calling his audience to
battle. One recurring theme is that the world, mainly
through liberal and revolutionary ideology, is attacking
the Church. To a large extent, this is the same battle
that the Church has always fought. There is, then, a
sense of eternal truth in these writings. His pastoral
theology reflects this truth as it applied to the lives of

---

18   Nicolas Casa in Jose David Cortes Guerrero, "Intransigencia y
nación. El discurso de Ezequiel Moreno y Nicolas Casas, Primeros
vicarios apostólicos del Casanare," in *Fronteras*, vol. 3 (1998), 205.
19   Angel Martinez Cuesta, *Ezequiel Moreno Santo de tres
continentes* (Madrid: Augustinus, 2006), 10.
20   Medina, 150.

everyone he ministered to. Nothing could have made the Catholic faith more relevant than this. This pastoral concern motivated his many pastoral visits throughout the diocese, and brought Fray Ezequiel close to the people.[21] He called the people to prayer, obedience to the Church, devotion to Mary and the Sacred Heart of Jesus, and other traditional Catholic practices.

Like any good pastoral theologian, Moreno-Díaz had a keen sense of the psychology of sin and of the road to salvation that envisions God and man working closely together. It is rooted in Augustinian theology in that it examines the effects of sin on the soul and on the psychological state of the human being. In one passage, St. Ezequiel first cites St. Paul's observations of the effects of sin on the person: "Who changed the truth of God into a lie; and worshiped and served the creature rather than the Creator, who is blessed for ever. Amen. For this cause God delivered them up to shameful affections... to a reprobate sense."[22] He then identifies how sin affects our relationship with God, and how this changed relationship in turn affects the sinner's psychology: "These words of the Apostle clearly express how God will abandon those who abandon him. This is the great punishment that God commands for the sinner. The major evidence of his just anger is that he permits that a sin be punished by another sin."

Moreno is strongest in this pastoral acumen because he speaks from experience. This experience provides him with a piercing gaze into human nature, particularly the havoc that sin wrecks on the soul. Yet he retains hope for redemption, even at this point:

> One single mortal sin is enough to bring death to this love, and killing this, the soul also dies. But this very sin, that kills this love and the

21 Ayape, 46.
22 Romans 1:25, 26, 28.

soul, cannot get to this faith that remains and subsists in the soul even though it is dead. It is the principle with which the grace of God can resuscitate it, and the root from which, with the same divine grace, the leafy tree of Christian holiness can once again sprout.

Moreno epitomizes the fearless, determined, truthful, and orthodox bishop who is willing to stand up for the faith and the faithful. What makes his writings so relevant for today is that he is the kind of bishop that the Catholic Church desperately needs right now. His words, though addressing the issues of the day in Colombia, are as timely as if they had been written yesterday. Moreno speaks to us about the travails and injustices that we are going through. His calling a spade a spade has a great impact on the reader:

> Many women are indeed accomplices to liberals according to one or another of the indicated methods. In this case, I pray to Our Lord Jesus Christ, that we do not go back to calling these women angels of peace, nor say that they are virtuous, nor praise their piety, because this is deception. They do more damage than if they burned down the houses they live in or damaged them. Mercy vociferously demands that we tell them that they are committing evil, that they are sinners, so that they repent, stop their sins of complicity, and beg God for forgiveness and the grace that they sin no more.

Such words support the claim that St. Ezequiel was "a pastor who felt obliged to point out the danger to his sheep with total clarity. He was not an intellectual, sitting at his desk, with the time to calmly analyze and dissect things."[23]

---

23   Cuesta, 14.

This directness explains the striking mixture of humility with self-confidence and assertiveness in these writings. The humility comes from St. Ezequiel's regard for himself, while his self-confidence stems from his absolute trust in the Lord and the Church. The core of Moreno's teaching and pastoral work reflects the simple belief that "the Catholic faith illuminates man."

He represents a militant, determined, and confident Church that speaks with boldness to the world, corrects vice, upholds virtue, and proclaims Jesus Christ to the world. He is supremely aware of the spiritual battle waged against his Church, and of the necessary type of response. This does not lead to clericalism, for, in his respect for the laity, he calls on them to do much of this fighting. His blunt statements about the Church's opponents, and instructions to the faithful on how to oppose these forces, were surely inspiring to his listeners and readers, as he calls them away from a comfortable faith:

> We likewise should also not marvel at the fact that declared enemies of Jesus Christ praised his teaching when they heard in it the voice of the truth: "The divine book of the Gospel (as some say) is the sole necessity for a Christian, and even more useful for those who are not. It requires nothing more than meditation in order to bring forth love in the soul for its author, and spark in it the desire to fulfil its teachings. Never had the truth been expressed with such a sweet and suggestive language, nor the most profound wisdom spoken with such an admirable energy and simplicity."[24] This praise from such a terrible enemy of our Divine Master, saves us the work of setting out other proofs to confirm that the doctrines of

---

24   The author attributes this to J. J. Rousseau, *Pensamientos*, 3, but it is unclear what book this is.

the Catholic faith perfect the life of man and
moralize his customs.

Fray Ezequiel unabashedly asserts the rights and doctrines of the Catholic Church. He submits to these doctrines and expects others to do so as well.

St. Ezequiel's insights are relevant for today. He
observes a special kind of desperation and *acedia* in people
who limit themselves to a this-world horizon:

> Today they are victims of horrible skepticism,
> without this resignation, without these hopes,
> without the comfort of this happy and bright
> future. They could not experience anything other
> than weariness, anguish, restlessness, despera-
> tion. And given that they have nothing more to
> aspire to than the joys of this life, if they do not
> have this, the logical consequence is that they
> search for this at any price and in every way,
> even criminal ways. From this results appall-
> ing revolutions, bloody battles, social troubles:
> communism, nihilism, anarchism, the use of
> dynamite. This sad and terrifying spectacle that
> everywhere promotes modern liberties frightens
> those who establish the principles that have
> such fatal consequences.

Such words sound oddly contemporary. Also oddly
contemporary is Moreno's warning about the information
war faced by the Church. At the beginning of the third
circular letter, he warns of the danger of the written
word, in this case concerning the letter of Baltasar Vélez.
This priest had "applauded the conciliatory attitude of
Carlos Martinez Silva."[25] Moreno was keenly aware of the
havoc that comes from the fact that once falsehoods are
circulated, they take on a life of their own. As with many
other insights of St. Ezequiel, this is timely for today.

---

25   Cuesta, 12.

St. Ezequiel's prescience about human rights as a weapon against the traditional religious order is equally impressive. Looking *back* over the past fifty or more years, we can conclude that human rights have been regularly exploited to attack the foundations of Christian society. They have helped establish abortion, divorce, polyamory, surrogate motherhood, and a host of other antichristian practices. Speaking decades before any of this came to pass, Fray Ezequiel opposed human rights on the grounds that liberals hide their destructive goals of social and family destruction behind human rights reasoning. Once again, he discerns the *spirit* of liberalism.

Because this spirit has not changed over the decades, much of St. Ezequiel's observations and admonitions remain fully relevant today. He examines the psychology of those who claim that they are being prudent peacemakers but who in fact lack courage. At times, his words sting the contemporary Catholic ear which has become so comfortable with platitudes that aim to avoid asserting the truth and that therefore fail to build meaningful or durable relationships, fail to prevent sin, and fail to succeed against the onslaught of the anti-Christian mindset. "Reverend priests, you must understand perfectly that there cannot be peace between the two armies, but only war," he warns.

By tracing the harmful influence of revolutionary or liberal society on the Christian soul, he demonstrates why this brave stance was so vital then, and continues to be so now, in how it ultimately affects each soul: "At the beginning, perhaps one does not approve of his evil insinuations, and even expresses disgust. But bit by bit, this disgust disappears, and then these are not even thought of as evil. Later, they are regarded as humorous events. Finally, they penetrate the entire soul, and come to occupy the same place that religious beliefs used to occupy." As a master psychologist, St. Ezequiel has a keen sense that humans are social animals, and that therefore what is presently circulating in society sooner or later finds its way into our souls if Christians fail to remain vigilant.

Despite the power of these writings, they seem to give us only a glimpse of the saint's holiness, at least if we are to consider eyewitness accounts. He was recognized as a living saint as early as his time in the Philippines, where "his parishioners took him to be a man of God and frequently declared him to be a saint... Neither in Las Piñas nor in Santo Tomás had people known such a parish priest, and when they sensed that he would soon be leaving them, they would become very upset and would petition the archbishop and the Recollect provincial to keep him for a while longer."[26] His close collaborator in Santo Tomás, Tomás Roldán, declared, "Father Ezequiel was a saint. He was an angel."[27] While these translations may give us a sense of knowing this saint, in fact his holiness seems to have been much more personal. These writings therefore offer us only a glimpse into this saint, however important and appealing that is. Hopefully, this book is only the beginning of a much greater awareness of the saintly life of St. Ezequiel.

26   Cuesta, 5.
27   Ayape, 27.

PASTORAL
LETTERS

FIRST
Pastoral Letter

THAT HIS EXCELLENCY
FR. EZEQUIEL MORENO DÍAZ
BISHOP OF PINARA AND
APOSTOLIC VICAR TO CASANARE,
ADDRESSED TO THE FAITHFUL
OF HIS VICARIATE.

*We, Fr. Ezequiel Moreno Díaz, from the Order of Hermits
of St. Augustine, through the grace of God and the Holy
See, Bishop of Pinara and Apostolic Vicar of Casanare
To our much-loved brothers in the religious missions, and
to all the faithful of our Vicariate, beloved sons in the
Lord: Greetings and blessings.*

*I am the light of the world.[1]
I am the way, the truth, and the life.[2]*

THUS SAID JESUS CHRIST OUR
Lord of himself. He is eternal Wisdom, the
Word of the Father who became human for
the salvation of men.

Here is the truth, my beloved children: Being thus
constituted, it is clear and most naturally spontaneous to
see that the happier and more joyful individuals, nations,
and societies are, the more correctly they proceed towards
their perfection, their true enlightenment, and their true
progress, and the nearer they are to Our Lord Jesus Christ.

---

1 John 8:12.
2 John 14:6.

He is the true path, to the light, to truth and life. On the contrary, the more miserable all their ideas are, the more enveloped they are in the darkness of error, the more lost and disoriented from the true path. This makes people more remote from him, from his holy doctrines, and from all light, truth, life.

That is what sane reason persuades us and what history demonstrates in the most eloquent way with its untold facts. One example will suffice. Africa shone when it was the homeland of Tertullian, Cyprian, Augustine, Alypius, and Fulgentius. This contrasts horribly with its current degradation and misery, with its sad submission and shameful manner of existence and life since it moved away from God, from the true Light, and the true Life, and buried itself in the darkness of death and suffering when the Quran and the Crescent spread everywhere.

We say this fact so often and as eloquently as a tongue can say it. But although history does not mention this nor leave any trace of it, like with a thousand other things, the slightest and simplest observation tells us this with the most persuasive eloquence. Poor people are distant from Jesus Christ, either because he was never proclaimed to them or because they apostatized from him. Such poor people are deprived of the priesthood, the holy sacrifice, worship, Christian teaching—in a word, they are deprived of everything that Jesus Christ instituted to guide men on the route to salvation, bliss, and happiness, and to draw them to him. He is the Light, the Truth, and the Life!

What do we observe in them? A horrendous anemia that consumes and annihilates them. A listlessness, a lack of courage and of vigor that leads them, like the unfortunate who are attacked by tuberculosis, towards a poor, rickety, and miserable existence that brings them closer to death at every instant. Maybe, just maybe, a religious sensibility survives in a few souls as a flicker that has not yet been extinguished. But this flicker, like the last remains of paper that has been burned, oscillates between dark ash and the dark cloak of death. This thought of Christ, wrapped up and surrounded by thick clouds of ignorance, mixed with thousands of preoccupations and errors, slumbers in fatal inaction and is totally unfruitful for good.

A striking example of this is Casanare ... Casanare! Casanare! The beautiful region of Casanare, prepared for Providence, shut up in your broad stronghold of populous cities that swim in abundance! How you are so alone! No one passes through your extensive plains that are free of obstacles for carriage wheels or the speed of steam engines. No one travels on your plentiful and picturesque rivers. You are so abandoned! No one exploits your fertility and riches. No one enjoys the varied singing of your birds nor the grace and beauty of your surprising and splendid vegetation. Ah! There was a time when the sweat of zealous missionaries watered your earth and made your land fruitful with their fatigue and hard work. This elevated you to the heights of civilization and prosperity, from which you should never have fallen. You were so beautiful and graceful then!

But not today. Who deprived you of this tireless effort that you worked with such passion and that brought such abundant fruits of Christian civilization and even material progress? Who snatched these heroic men away from your soil? Filled with such charity and selflessness, they left the imprints of their beneficial and civilizing progress everywhere. Oh! Guard! Guard carefully in your dense forests the ruins of your people, your buildings, your wonderful churches ... that they always lift up with their singing voices the glories of the missionaries, and reproach and condemn those who took from you and were the cause of your desolation and misfortune.

We contemplate you when we see you. You are like a widow who has lost her spouse, crying over your happy past, lamenting your unfortunate present, sensing your lack of force and life, and waiting sadly for your inevitable future death if no one comes to grieve with you over your situation and bring you Catholicism's invigorating breath. This breath renews everything and gives warmth to all of life.

But . . . God be praised! The appointed time of divine Providence has already arrived for you. The time of great mercy draws near, and you can already see the cheerful dawn of a promising future.

Citizens of Casanare, you are not forgotten. You are neither alone nor abandoned. Government workers, as honorable authorities, feel in their hearts the rejuvenating faith of Catholicism and are moved by its impulses. They recognize its necessity and seek its support. They understand that life and progress are only possible with the teachings of Jesus Christ. You citizens cannot remain indifferent to the great disgrace that afflicts your territory. Wanting more than this, you look around yourselves and have erected wise laws to raise you from this prostration to the higher path of progress that your advantageous conditions call you to.

In order to fulfill these laws, the nation's government sent worthy authorities along with intelligent clerks to keep order, preserve the rightful place of morals, and promote material advancement. But knowing that all of this was insufficient, they worked with His Excellency, the apostolic delegate, who by his efforts brought you spiritual aid and therefore will always deserve your gratitude. This led to the Holy See designating an apostolic vicar at the level of bishop. This vicar became the spiritual leader of the entire physical area outlined by the current *intendencia*.[3]

This appointment fell to my humble person. Obligated by this clear mandate given by my superiors, I accepted it. I was fearful of resisting the holy will of the Lord, which is the sole rule of all of our actions. Considering ourselves inexpressibly fortunate, we reflected on whether we could fulfill the thinking and plans of those who had wanted the Holy See to place us in this position of which we are not deserving. We will be so joyous if we are able to fulfill the mission that our Holy Father Leo XIII deigned to confide to our weaknesses! And what is this mission? To what end have I come to Casanare? Let me tell you with the greatest clarity that I possibly can.

Our Lord Jesus Christ, the great One sent by the heavenly Father to teach men the path to salvation and the way to serve and worship him in *spirit and truth*, declared himself to be the sole Master of humanity. He said this in a clear and definitive way: *Magister unus est Christus*.[4] Despite this declaration, he wanted his direct teaching to be given to deputies. To this end, he instituted a body of those sent out with the commission to teach all men. He said to his apostles, "Going therefore, teach ye all nations; baptizing them in the name of the Father, and of the Son, and of the Holy Ghost. Teaching them to observe all things whatsoever I have commanded you: and behold I am with you all days, even to the consummation of the world."

This is what the Divine Master said. These words have the same power and effectiveness as all words that came from the mouth of God. They are heard today and resonate with the same power and intensity as when he spoke

---

3   Colombia was formerly divided into administrative districts called *intendencias*.

4   "You have one master" (Matt. 23:10).

them the first time when he launched the brave apostles and other disciples on the spiritual conquest of the world. After these apostles came their successors in the teaching office and pastorate, and after them a multitude of others were also sent out. Nothing stopped the advance: *"always beautiful like those of the messenger of good and of peace,"*[5] in order to bring his word and preaching to the ends of the world: *in omnem terram exivit sonus eorum, et in fines orbis terrae verba eorum.*[6] Not even the most furious persecutions, harshest penalties, or cruelest martyrdoms stopped them and the Cross, the Cross which was wet with the divine blood that was spilled at Calvary; the Cross, the sign and summary of all divine teachings, gloriously and triumphantly covering the whole world, *renewing the world's face,*[7] and transforming the moral world undoubtedly more miraculously than the first light that followed the divine *fiat* that transformed the dark chaos.

A new reign of virtue, justice, and saintliness was established everywhere. This was a new order of things that the world had not seen before. It was divine in its origin, unchanging in its essence, and sublime in its goal of man's worldly and eternal bliss. The world was amazed and wonderstruck when it heard the preaching of unknown doctrines, which included a humble heart, chastity, meekness, acceptance of adversity, forgiveness of sins, compassion for the unfortunate, and all of these virtues that ennoble man, purify his emotions, and sanctify all the states, ages, and conditions. They equally heard the following great truth from the mouths of those who were sent by God, that all men are brothers, that there is no distinction between the slave and the freeman, rich and poor, or Jew and Greek, because everyone has *the one*

5   Isa. 52:7.
6   Ps. 18:5.
7   Ps. 103:32.

same God who is the Father of all,[8] and that everyone has the right to the inheritance of their one Father. The world feels regenerated and awoken to new life with these sublime doctrines. The people sent by God clear the way to a sweet and perfect civilization of true brotherhood with these maxims and teachings, which are so humanitarian and social. They proclaim equality before the law, outline the positive rights of man, and signal his duties towards God, himself, his brothers, and, as a consequence, society.

This was such an amazing transformation! The most ferocious instincts were softened, passions were tamed, codes and laws were Christianized, servants were emancipated, the poor were raised up, the homeless were given shelter, women were rehabilitated and exalted, legalized prostitution and other excesses that were allowed by previous legislation were abolished, and brotherly love was established among men and even included enemies. What more? Who can say what those sent by Christ accomplished in the world by carrying before themselves the doctrine of the Cross, the true light of the world, the way, the truth, and the life? They spoke, and this voice civilized the barbarian. The savage, the Scythian, the man of the woods, and the nomad of the deserts gave up the wandering life, the wild life, to enjoy a range of distinctions among men of spiritual freedom, rights, hope, and happiness unknown before. They spoke, and worked wonders of holiness and true civilization everywhere, always going to the highest level of things. They initiated the most glorious enterprises, taking the principal part in them and always connecting them with the most brilliant thinkers, and working for good wherever they went. The same living witness to their work existed in India, Japan, and China, along with the glowing African earth, America's untouched forests, and Oceana's remotest islands.

---

8   Rom. 9:12.

Beloved sons and brothers, these are the benefits and sublime missions that those sent by the Lord brought everywhere. We, one of those sent even though unworthy, cannot bring anything else to you. We are here to teach you the same heavenly doctrine, all the fundamental dogmas that make up the soul of the moral universe, that God made known so that man would know where he comes from, where he is going, and what he must believe, hope, and fear.

We will remind you of these great truths of time and eternity, virtue and reward, sin and punishment. We will explain the precepts that God Our Lord gave to men, and how their blessed and eternal future depends on observing these. We will preach to them the love of God, charity for the neighbor, obedience to superiors, respect for law, diligence at work, and, indeed, all of the sublime teachings of Jesus Christ that, along with those whom he sent, changed the face of the earth in bringing forth the happiest moral revolution. Only this teaching is capable of developing virtuous parents, obedient children, faithful spouses, honorable subordinates, and peaceful citizens who produce peace, well-being, and the advancement of the people. At the same time, this teaching leads individuals to the ends for which they were created and enables them to reach the crown of glory.

We will also bind and set free, absolve and condemn, correct bad customs, speak out against public sins, and point out bad pastures, so that the sheep that we have been given are not thus fed with such things. We will warn about the wolves that want to devour them, and defend the sheep from them, even when this requires us to give our own life, because *the good shepherd gives his life for his sheep*, says our Lord Jesus Christ.[9] My children, you have been without priests to instruct you in the doctrines

9   John 10:11.

of the gospel, without apostles of the truth, without missionaries from the Lord. However, apostles of error and missionaries of Satan did not appear to be lacking. They exaggerated your rights and promised deceitful and made-up prosperity, only wanting you to shake off Catholicism's gentle yoke. They wanted you to chase after every new wind of doctrine and to embrace modern errors which have been condemned many times by our mother Church. Do not let yourself be seduced by the false apostles who seek the destruction of your souls and want you to listen not to priests, but to them. They try to stop you from being faithful children of the Church so that you can be their disciples and serve them and their miserable purposes, under the pretense of doing good, so that you can become rooted in the world of deception and idle pleasures.

We also come to you to always be at your side, like a good father is at the side of his sons, to be on the lookout for your well-being, assisting you in your necessities and encouraging you with words and, much more, with our good example in walking the paths of Christian perfection. We will travel the length and breadth of your extensive territory to administer the sacraments, ensure the splendor of the liturgy, correct the abuses that can occur in this territory, form pious practices, and signal to all the paths of eternal salvation. Extreme heat, torrential downpours, the difficulty of the journey, the distance from place to place, and other hardships are not excuses for us in failing to fulfill these tasks.

We are invested with the authority of Jesus Christ in order to carry out the responsibilities that we have mentioned. *There is only one sheepfold and one shepherd.*[10] All the pastors of the Catholic Church comprise one single pastor with the adorable person of Our Lord Jesus Christ. When we baptize, when we consecrate, when

---

10   John 10:16.

we absolve, it is Jesus Christ who baptizes, consecrates, and absolves, as my great Father St. Augustine says.[11] In all of our pastoral functions, we take the place of Jesus Christ. Just as *God was in Jesus Christ to reconcile the world*,[12] so Jesus Christ is in the pastors who continue the great work of redemption of the human race. About this Jesus Christ said, "*Whoever hears you, hears me; whoever despises you, despises me; and whoever despises me despises he who sent me.*[13] Our authority over your souls is the authority of Jesus Christ himself. This means that whoever resists anything in our ministry does not resist man, but Jesus Christ himself.

Do not think that when we speak this way we elevate ourselves and show off our dignity. Ah! We cannot think of this dignity without exclaiming with David: *Exaltatus autem, humiliatus sum, et conturbatus.*[14] To be elevated to the dignity with which we are invested, we are humbled and filled with worry in considering the overwhelming weight of our charge, our great responsibility, and the narrow and rigorous account to which we are held by the Supreme Pastor of souls. No, we do not put ourselves above you, but tremble in your presence and suffer to bring about your salvation.

We believe that no one thinks that we have come to Casanare for worldly motives. However, for those who imagine such things, we are happy that we cannot expect a palace or comfortable house to live in, or an enormous income to enrich ourselves, or abundant and fine dining, or the means for comfortable and pleasant living.

We are happy that none of this awaits us because no one can say or even suppose that we are led here out of

---

11   Tract. 5 in John.
12   2 Cor. 5:19.
13   Lk. 10:16.
14   Ps. 87:16.

ambition, avarice, well-being, or other worldly motive, but only for the sublime and elevated objective of giving glory to God, illuminating your intelligences with the light of faith, embellishing your hearts with the Christian virtues, achieving, in a nutshell, the eternal salvation of your souls.

We know perfectly what people here hope, because we have already experienced it. We know that, in addition to the moral suffering from our charge, we will spend many days traveling around your hot land with no more food than a poor Indian, and sometimes without even that due to accidents that are never lacking. We will spend many nights with no more than the sand of the beaches of your rivers as a bed, close—so many times!—close to voracious caimans...and with only the clouds of the firmament to cover us. Those clouds often brought heavy rains that, in addition to tormenting us, lead to fatal fevers that bring down the healthiest, if not kill them, as so often happens. This is what awaits us: poverty, scarcity, work, sacrifice, and the cross—aa large and heavy cross. We have come, then, to suffer for the salvation of your souls. The salvation of your souls! That is, my sons, the goal that has brought us here, the motive that pushes us towards the hard company that we have taken unto ourselves. If this were not so, if we did not meditate on the glory of God and your eternal salvation...ah! With all the sincerity of our heart, we confess to you: Our personal interest, our health, the civilized society that surrounds us, the good friendships that honor and distinguish us ...everything, everything, in a word, in a loud voice, we should leave them with respect to religious things, in your plains and forests because here or elsewhere we are with greater comfort, with more resources, more social interactions, greater means, to say it more simply, to live a more comfortable and pleasant life. This is so clear and obvious, that nothing more needs to be said.

Very well, my beloved sons, if only we can lead you to a greater interest in your souls, in your eternal salvation, make sure—let me say it to you as Saint Peter Chrysologus said to his people (then for your spiritual salvation, like him, I did not refuse to take on this heavy burden)—make sure to take advantage of our ministry, our mission, the purpose, indeed, for which God has sent us here. For in having given this ministry, at the same time he made you worthy of the mercy of God, and to achieve his plans for your eternal salvation. He who has prepared for us indescribable joy lightens our load and makes us forget our hurts—just like a mother forgets the pains of birth when her child is born and is placed at her breasts.

St. Paul writes, "Obey your prelates, and be subject to them. For they watch as being to render an account of your souls; that they may do this with joy, and not with grief. For this is not expedient for you."[15] Make sure, then, to take the fruit of our ministry so that we can provide this joy. But above all, because this interests you since it is your own salvation, your eternal happiness. Because if you do not seize this, you will be so pathetic. You alone will be responsible, and not God, because God, my brother, does not need to be worshiped and can very well exist without you. There is no lack of souls on whom can be poured the torrents of his mercy. Because if he so chooses, he can convert the stones themselves into sons of Abraham who will worship him in full faith. The Word of God must, on the other hand, not be unfruitful, because it is written: *verbum meum, quod egredietur de ore meo, non revertetur ad me vacuum, sed ... prosperabitur in his, ad quae missi illud.*[16] As we are sent by God, we

---

15 Heb. 13:17.
16 Isa. 55:11.

want to announce to you with insistence given to us by the Apostle, with the confidence of a happy result if not in some, than in others; if not with the conversion and sanctification of those already in the Church, then in those who until now have not had the chance. For God called us to this, and spoke to our heart. But if people despise this and don't hear it, and go forward alone, to whom will they go? Keep in mind that we are also sent to the unbelieving who are among you.

The unbelieving! The savages! Yes, we are also sent to these unfortunate people because the Catholic Church was established to illuminate the entire universe through its ministers, without recognizing any privileges, without conditions for any class, without showing special favors, and for the poorest and most in need. The world does not consider the savages. Most men look on them with disdain and rude scorn, if they do not pursue and kill them like harmful animals. The same people who call themselves friends of humanity, *phi ...lan ...thropes* (*cymbalum tiniens*). These same men have never thought of doing good towards the savages. Take notice, as a wise writer observes, that none of them have shed a drop of blood in Japan or China to remove barbarism.

The Catholic Church, in contrast, provides for their hearts, even at the cost of the missionaries' sweat, sacrifice, and even lives. These missionaries seek to give them faith, civilization, and heaven itself. Ah! No, no faith community, sect, or society does this, no matter how philanthropic they declare themselves to be. The Catholic Church alone does these things. Through these works, apostolic Rome provides a brilliant example of itself as a divine institution because God, and God alone, can inspire it to provide to the whole world, to all peoples, the doctrine of eternal salvation. Only God can make this work universal.

The Lord Jesus Christ declares, "And other sheep I have, that are not of this fold: them also I must bring, and they shall hear my voice, and there shall be one fold and one shepherd." *Et alias oves habeo ...et fiet unum ovile et unus pastor.*[17] We will make these words of the Good Shepherd and his loving desires our own, and in reference to Casanare's unbelieving. A great part of our attention, care, and sleepless nights will focus on them. We will make so many sacrifices for them in order to instruct, civilize, and save them. Ah! If only I could exhale my last breath in a poor straw hut, or on a sandy beach, or at the foot of a tree, and could say, "There are no unbelievers in Casanare!" Their numbers are not very high according to what the missionary fathers tell us in their letters, but their unity and conversion are no small difficulties. The main and most numerous tribes, such as the Guahibos, are nomadic and without fixed residence. Nevertheless, God's mercy is great, and we hope that he gives us a few souls in exchange for the hardship and sacrifices. We will seek to unite them with the Precious Blood and the great Sacrifice of our Divine Redemptor.

Large, spacious, and so vast is the field that God has granted us in our zeal. Large in its expansion, but larger even is the great shortage of the means to help the people. We anticipate thousands of souls that are already Christian, and we do not have enough apostolic workers to care for all of their necessities. It would be necessary to reach out to them and train them, or better to reach out to some and to train others, according to what is possible. We need to put up buildings for the education and preparation of these, as well as accommodations for the missionaries. The co-workers that God has sent us need decent clothing. Churches need to be built and decorated in the best manner possible, including ornaments

---

17   John 10:16.

and sacred vessels. We must find resources that will attract the unbelievers. Indeed, we have a great deal of work ahead of us.

But how? With what means? Who will help me? Sacred Heart of Jesus, I turn to you! I put all my hope in you. You will be my help, my treasure, my wisdom, my strength, and my refuge. *Fortitudo mea, et refugium meum es Tu.*[18] These are the words that surround the Sacred Heart of Jesus, that we declare to be the seal of our office. They will constantly remind us that, not trusting in ourselves, we have confided everything to the Sacred Heart, that has in all times, including today, carried out countless miracles of love, and that has the power to do so in the future. These words will be a continuous and powerful stimulation so that this Sacred Heart will reign everywhere—in families, peoples, and nations—and fill everyone with his sovereign influence. This includes his lordship over our whole vicariate, that he reigns fully over all of it, that the vicariate be his, totally his, and always his. These words will also be the help and support of our weakness, speaking to us at every moment that, no matter how weak our knowledge and virtue, we will not falter; that this Sacred Heart, that in every era aided the weak and the suffering to make them ambassadors of his holy will and to bring about the most stupendous miracles for the good of souls. The Sacred Heart can also use us, as docile instruments, to achieve his providential designs. What those are, we do not know. We do not know for whom our mission will be effective, or who will benefit from it. But we know that as long as we have total confidence in the Sacred Heart of Jesus . . . the work will not be useless. The work will be happy and beneficial. Thus, we confidently expect help from God, and are convinced, with the great apostle when he said,

---

18   Ps. 30:4.

"neither the one who plants, nor the one who waters is anything, but only God who makes things grow."[19]

But as we are also convinced that this help comes from heaven through prayer, we ask for prayers, as the apostle did from the faithful in his epistles, saying time and again: pray for me, my brothers; pray for my works, pray for my preaching, pray that it spreads the sacred word. Pious souls! To you I turn in particular: And how your heart must understand what I desire! There are souls that, to be of God, wait for your prayers. From these, perhaps, depend their conversion and salvation. Offer a few prayers, along with some deprivation and penance, some alms, in order to provide the benefits of the faith that God has already given you in his mercy. By that alone, you will take an abundant part in the sacrifices of the missionaries. These heroes, abandoning the costliest and nicest things of this world for these sacrifices, have headed into the forests to spread the light of the gospel. These apostolic men also need your prayers and your help so that their words bear fruit in souls. Help them with this, so that in this way, without leaving your houses, you can win souls with them, and make shine on your faces the reflection of this aureola of glory that crowned the propagators of the faith. Pray, then, for the souls, pray for the missionaries, and also pray to the Lord of the harvest to send more workers, as they are always few, very few.

And I greet you, my dear brothers, until the day comes when I can embrace you tenderly and lovingly. I know your deeds. I know your works. I am not unaware that you have suffered hunger, thirst, heat, poverty, want of every kind, loneliness, and illnesses that brought you to the edge of the grave. I, who have followed with my spirit these magnificent apostolic works, cannot find the words to describe, to fathom, to praise them, because there are

---

19   1 Cor. 3:7

things that exceed the power of words. The world does not see any of this, and does not know how to appreciate these sacrifices, this life of abnegation, deprivation, and hardships. This life renounces all comfort, all human interaction, all naturalness. This life is one of constant solitude. It is completely forgotten, shares only the company of wild men, and suffers their incivility, ignorance, misery, nauseating side, and, the most painful of all, their ingratitude.

No, the world does not know how to appreciate all of this. But, ah! God, my brothers, appreciates it in all its worth. And his angels write down every step of your beautiful feet, and record each one of your sufferings so that not one of you is left without eternal reward.

It has been three years since we put you in this solitude, and you have this advantage over us; three years of merit and glory, three years, my brothers, that have already passed ... Ah! Life passes, and if it is offered in suffering for God, this is the only thing that is left; for suffering for God, for virtue, is the only currency that is valid in heaven. We are going to take part in that aspect of your service. Soon we will see each other and will find consolation in the Lord.

Sisters of Charity, daughters who are much-beloved in the Lord: You have also preceded us in coming to accumulate merits in this land, where there is so much need to exercise the offices of charity that are a part of your Institute. You have already begun to work, and wish to extend your beneficial work, and do as much as you can for the glory of God. I greet you affectionately. You can count on our affection for Jesus Christ, on our protection, on our help. Be secure in the interest that we have in watching everything that relates to the best fulfillment of your mission, and, above all, with your own sanctification.

People of Casanare, my much-beloved children: receive also our gentle greeting, the gentle greeting of a father, because God has determined that I be the father of your souls. You already know that I am the poor, undemanding missionary who visited you three years ago and who was content with your *cazabe*,[20] your plantain, or whatever you had to offer in exchange for the pleasure with which he served you in all that was connected to the well-being of your souls.

We are more elevated than before, but we don't therefore come to you with more pretensions. We have only the most ardent wish to win you for God and love you in God. And who can I love, if not you? Ah! You'll be the apples of my eye because Jesus has directed me to care for you and save you. Soon I will be with you and won't leave you. And my freedom, my time, my peace, my health, my life, all is yours, and I am ready to sacrifice this for your well-being.

My children, I wish to give Jesus Christ to all of you with humility, meekness, and all the virtues that belong to the sheep that hear his voice, so that one day you will be at his right hand and will be taken to the kingdom of glory. I wish for that with all my heart.

Let the blessing that I give you be a pledge of this blissful future for all, in the name of the Father ✠ and of the Son ✠ and of the Holy Spirit ✠. Amen.

Given and signed by us, and stamped with
our seal in Bogotá, the day of our consecration,
the first of May, eighteen hundred and ninety-four.
✠ Br. Ezequiel, *Bishop of Pinara and
Apostolic Vicar of Casanare.*

---

20   Unleavened bread from manioc flour.

FIRST
Pastoral Letter
(Pasto)

THAT HIS EXCELLENCY
FR. EZEQUIEL MORENO DÍAZ
BISHOP OF PASTO ADDRESSES HIS
DIOCESE, ENCOURAGING THEM TO
REMAIN FIRM IN THE FAITH AND
BE ALWAYS VIGILANT AGAINST
EVERY KIND OF SEDUCTION.

We, Fr. Ezequiel Moreno Díaz, from the Order of Hermits of St. Augustine, through the grace of God and the Holy See, Bishop of Pasto
To the venerable clergy and faithful of our Diocese, greetings and blessings in our Lord Jesus Christ.

WHEN WE WENT TO CASANARE to exercise our ministry as apostolic vicar in that territory, we could not imagine that we would have to leave before even two years. We were under the firm conviction that we would be staying in that region until our death, and in the absolute belief that from this poor dwelling, or from the beaches of its rivers, or from the thickness of its forests, we would pass to eternity and present ourselves before Jesus Christ in this way, shielded with the humble life that, despite our high dignity, we had to lead. And we would defend ourselves with the deprivations and work that we took upon ourselves, to obtain as much as possible the eternal salvation of our flock that is scattered throughout an extensive area, and that has been unhealthy until now because resources are scarce but inconveniences and dangers are not.

We must say in our naïvety that this idea of passing to the next life after a few years of poverty, deprivation, and suffering always pleased us in our time of meditation on our eternal future. And for this reason, when we received the notice of our transfer, the following question occurred to us: "Have we become unworthy to suffer for our Lord God? We are unworthy indeed of such bliss. But we do not know if this is the motive that moved the Lord to permit our transfer. What we know for certain is that we did not strive for or look for this, and that when we learned that we were being transferred, everything had already been set. In our sole desire to fulfill in ourselves the will of God in all things, we dared not put up the only possible appeal, which would be total resistance.

Still, many reasons raced through our head that seemed to justify making at least a few points in favor of staying where we were. We have to abandon a recently-begun work at which we believed we would be working until our death; abandon the missionary life that we saw ourselves adopting and that was so fitting with our inclinations; say goodbye with wishes of heaven to our brothers in this work with whom we could even live in community as we had always lived. Instead of this, we had to take on an even heavier, more delicate charge with more compromises and, above all, more responsibility before the Supreme Judge. The image of the eminent Msgr. Velasco,[1] with all of his virtues, knowledge, fame, and glory came before us. And considering that many of those who had the bliss of being governed by him are still alive, it occurred to us that it would be impossible to satisfy

1   Ignacio León Velasco S. J., fourth bishop of Pasto from 1889. He died in 1891 while serving as archbishop of Bogotá.

them, as they would necessarily make a comparison. This would result in the most accentuated contrast between his great gifts and our insufficiency. He who led the destiny of this diocese had the most outstanding personality filled with the most loving attributes of a pastor. When we viewed him, we felt forced to say: "You cannot fill the emptiness that he left behind; in this exchange, the diocese of Pasto will lose the faithful."

On the basis of what has been said, and so we understand each other perfectly, my children, seeing that you would lose much in the exchange, but without meaning to oppose the holy will of God in even the smallest thing, we still tried to stay where we were, and so in this way give you a more intelligent, zealous, honorable, and capable pastor to take the place of such an honorable predecessor.

It was all in vain. In the consistory of December 2 of last year, our Holy Father Pope Leo XIII followed the elevated and venerable judgment of our Lord God and publicly announced us as bishop of this diocese. Since then, only one thing remains for us to do, which is to humbly abide by the will of God and say with great submissiveness, "Let your holy will be done, Lord!"

We felt more than a little joy in our souls when we discovered that faith in Jesus Christ remains alive among you, and that this faith inspires, leads, and governs you. Being thus, we do not have to fear any more that you will look at our poor personality without any merit, except in that we are the one sent by God, the representative of Jesus Christ. We are the continuator of his sublime ministry, that which comes to exercise its functions among you. We know that you are always accustomed to looking at your bishops in this way. We know that you looked with the eyes of faith in this way, and seeing the lofty position of its ministry, you respected, obeyed, and loved it. With this background, we must hope that you will look with the same respect on us because it is Jesus Christ who directs this, and Jesus Christ is ever the same.

We therefore do not need to explain the functions that we must carry out among you, as the knowledge that you hold of these is the cause of the veneration and respect that you have always shown to your pastors. What should we say, then, in this first pastoral letter to you? We speak to you with the words of the apostle to the Colossians: "For though I be absent in body, yet in spirit I am with you; rejoicing, and beholding your order, and the steadfastness of your faith which is in Christ. As therefore you have received Jesus Christ the Lord, walk ye in him; rooted and built up in him, and confirmed in the faith, as also you have learned, abounding in him in thanksgiving. Beware lest any man cheat you by philosophy, and vain deceit; according to the tradition of men, according to the elements of the world, and not according to Christ."[2]

In these lofty words we find all that we want to say to you, namely two things. The first is that you remain steadfast and even grow in the faith, being thankful towards God for this great deed because he is the only way to bliss for the individual and society. The second is that you remain vigilant that you are not seduced by those who preach a philosophy that is false and contrary to the teachings of the Catholic faith, because these seducers bring ruin, blood, and desolation. Listen, therefore, to the call of your new pastor. The words of one are inspiration, those of the other are a warning.

I

Every Catholic knows that faith is necessary for eternal salvation because Jesus Christ said clearly and categorically that "he that believeth not shall be condemned."[3] Faith is

---

2   Col. 2:5–8.
3   Mark 16:16.

the first condition in moving closer to God. "Without faith it is impossible to please God,"[4] asserts the apostle. The Holy Council of Trent states that "faith is the beginning, foundation, and root of our justification."[5] The Vatican Council refers to this declaration from Trent, declaring: "Faith is the beginning of man's salvation according to the profession of the Catholic Church."[6] According to this doctrine, we cannot do meritorious works for heaven if faith does not spring forth from its roots, if these works do not come from faith as its beginning, and if they are not supported from this in their foundation.

Faith is not the work of man, but a gift from God, as the Church declares in the Council of Orange[7] and as the Vatican Council also taught.[8] This gift from God, according to my great Father St. Augustine, is worth more than all the treasures and things of this world. How we need to thank God for giving this to us! This precious gift is not only necessary for us to obtain eternal goods, but also to provide us with the happiness that is possible for us to find in this world that is filled with misery and sorrow. The Catholic Church's enemies have dared to say that faith harms the perfection of man. This error, which was so justly condemned in the *Syllabus*, was nevertheless disproved and condemned by history and experience. These both prove to us in the most convincing manner that the Catholic faith illuminates men and conveys knowledge that he could not reach on his own accord, perfects his life, moralizes his customs, alleviates and aids his misfortunes, and, in this way, exercises the most beneficial influence over society itself.

---

4   Heb. 11:6.
5   Session 6, Chapter 8.
6   Dogmatic Constitution "Dei Filius," Chapter 3, De fide.
7   Canon 5.
8   Dogmatic Constitution "Dei Filius," Chapter 3, De fide.

The Catholic faith illuminates man. In order to understand something of the illumination that the faith communicated to human intelligence, we only have to recall the times that preceded the proclamation of the gospel and see the monstrous errors that were dissipated by its radiant and beautiful light.

We Catholics, who have the joy to have been born in the bosom of the true Church of Jesus Christ and to have been brought up and educated by her, are illuminated by the faith from childhood. This education has given us more elevated ideas regarding God, his attributes, his works, his relations with creatures, and our obligations towards him, towards ourselves, and towards our neighbors. We do not properly value the bright light that the faith communicates to our understanding. We may even attribute to human endeavors a great deal of knowledge that is due solely to divine revelation. In then consulting history, we are amazed when we come across the beneficial influence that the faith exercised on the intellect, and we appreciate even more than normally this great gift of God.

History reveals that the pagan world was wrapped up in the most absurd errors, incredible delusions, and monstrous aberrations. Human reason could grasp certain truths, including the existence of one God. Nonetheless, the entire world was idolatrous except for the Hebrew nation. This nation adored the one true God because it had been illuminated through revelation. Without the aid of the faith, man saw gods in everything and everywhere. Man saw them in the stars that rotated in the firmament, in the animals that covered the Earth, and in the plants that sprouted up from her. As if there still were not enough gods, he made more from stones, wood, or metals. In his degradation, he paid the tribute to creatures that he owes solely to the Creator. But he felt fear and trembled before the piece of wood, stone, or bronze that he himself had made into God. The terrible idolatry took hold of the world. No one was free of the universal contagion: neither the people who had a flourishing literature and human sciences, nor those who appeared civilized, nor those who presented themselves as serious and earnest in their laws and institutions.

If these men held such erroneous ideas about the divinity, their ideas concerning other truths were no less absurd, above all regarding moral duties. There is no need to provide evidence for this point, because everyone knows the pagan customs. No one is ignorant of the fact that they divinized the passions themselves. They made each one into a god with its own altar, where it received low, degrading, and horribly bad worship. Their festivals were excesses of license and barbarism in honor of the gods. Modesty does not allow the reporting of such extravagant monstrosities.

And what is the source of the light that would come with sufficient force to dissipate such thick darkness? Human reason? No. Before the proclamation of the gospel, the world had already seen men who even today are called wise; there had already existed men who even today are considered to be great philosophers. Yet despite their wisdom, the world remained in the same darkness regarding God and morality. Men followed idolatrous and vicious beings, and each day more and more became submerged in the abyss of ignorance, superstition, immorality, and barbarity. Men—even the wisest—showed themselves incapable of illuminating the people and lifting them out of the obscurity and degradation in which they found themselves. Only God was able to provide a remedy to the universal loss of intelligence.

In his mercy, he came to do that by preaching the new law and being "the true light, which enlighteneth every man."[9] He helped them see their errors and depart from them. The doctrine of one God was presented in its full splendor, and the vividness of its light destroyed the darkness that was engulfed in false gods. Men could now see clearly that they were merely human creatures. They were scorned, as they deserved. They fell, little by little, from their magnificent pedestals. With the same brilliance, a great truth of a future life was presented, with its rewards and punishments. This put a brake on vice and encouraged virtue. No less clear were all the other important and lofty truths that Jesus Christ predicted, with which man was elevated from his prostration and which made known to him his origin, his earthly destiny, and his future.

The gospel and ensuing faith gave men knowledge that they would never have arrived at independently, even if they all possessed extraordinary talent and dedicated themselves exclusively to study. The most admirable thing is that such lofty understanding, sublime knowledge, and wisdom that surpasses the wisdom of the few men who were called wise in antiquity, spread throughout the social classes to even the most unfortunate and humble. Faith enlightened the people more than the most renowned pagan philosophers did. For this reason, Minucius Felix exclaimed: "It appears that all the Christians were true philosophers, or that all the philosophers became Christian."[10] The faith therefore enlightened men. But is this the only thing that it did? No, it is not only this. It also perfected their lives and moralized their customs.

---

9   John 1:9.
10   Octavius, Chapter XX.

III

If, as already stated, the faith dissipates absurd errors and illuminates human reason, it is no less certain that it destroys terrible vices and improves customs. A new way of life was seen in the world with the preaching of the gospel. The Bacchanales, the Saturnalia, and other pagan festivals, which were nothing other than the manifestations of effeminacy, corruption, licentiousness, and vice, were replaced by other, entirely contrary customs, in which temperance, purity, honesty, meekness, and other no less beautiful virtues shone. This fact is universally recognized since the great open book of history is available to everyone.

The doctrine of the Catholic faith is the highest, purest, and holiest. It alone has at its disposal sufficient means to elevate man to a perfection that is not possible to explain, but that, nevertheless, amazes, enchants, and carries him off. It commands us to direct all things to God, the Lord and Owner of all things. The soul has its powers just as the body has the senses. All that man has and does — his thoughts, wishes, actions — all must refer to God, without permitting even the smallest thing that has not been purified with this right, beautiful, and saintly intention.

According to this great precept, the greatest of all, the Catholic religion makes it immediately compulsory to love our neighbors. In order that this love be expressed and that the needs of others be met, the Catholic religion commands certain things under the weight of sin, and advises others under the promise of reward. No one is ignorant of the sublime precepts to love even our enemies and to give alms and other things for the well-being of our neighbors. And everyone knows the good and beautiful that are contained in works of mercy, as taught by the Christian catechism, that allow men to be well-provided for in all the needs of body and soul.

The Catholic Church, in addition, decrees precepts that are suitable for all social conditions and classes. It gives rules to those whom it governs and those who must obey—to fathers, sons, spouses, supervisors, servants, the well-to-do, the poor. The Church requires mutual service among these groups and considerations of charity for all. So that there is incentive to practice what each one is ordered, and so each lives according to his situation without envy, mistrust, rancor, or ill will, heaven invites everyone to its eternal happiness as a precious and common inheritance. The Catholic religion does not abandon any individual or leave him without the means to become virtuous, perfect, and holy. If everyone fulfills the precepts of our beloved religion, everyone will be holy. Those who fulfilled it had no need of legal punishments, or prisons, or armies to guard public order because this order was never disturbed.

It is therefore not surprising that the Jews themselves were astonished many times by the lofty doctrine of the gospel, by what came out of the Savior's divine lips, and by what that others enthusiastically confessed when they said, "Never did man speak like this man."[11] We likewise should not marvel at the fact that declared enemies of Jesus Christ praised his teaching when they heard in it the voice of the truth: "The divine book of the gospel (as some say) is the sole necessity for a Christian, and even more useful for those who are not. It requires nothing more than meditation in order to bring forth love in the soul for its author, and spark in it the desire to fulfill its teachings. Never had the truth been expressed with such a sweet and suggestive language, nor the most profound wisdom spoken with such an admirable energy

11 John 7:46 (Luke 4:22–32 is given in the original Spanish text).

and simplicity."[12] This praise from such a terrible enemy of our Divine Master, saves us the work of setting out other proofs to confirm that the doctrines of the Catholic faith perfect the life of man and moralize his customs.

IV

For every class of men, the Catholic faith is a blessing from God that cannot be properly appreciated. This very faith appears as an even greater blessing for the poor, the miserable, and those who suffer and are unfortunate. With its dogmas, it elevates the thinking of the miserable. It helps them see how much conformity with divine precepts pleases the Lord. It helps them understand that each instant of pain merits an eternal reward. It shows them heaven as the end of their suffering and beginning of endless joy. These teachings not only sweeten suffering, but also elevate man to the point of desiring them, seeking them, asking for them, and even finding solace in them. St. Paul says "that I was overflowing with joy in the middle of tribulations."[13] Catholic doctrine does this. It achieves this in many souls and deepens its consoling dogmas through meditation. There is also no lack of resources to alleviate the troubles of those who have not arrived at such virtue. These resources inspire these, in the least, to submission, and also helps them with the charity of the good faithful.

It is a fact that the Catholic religion has from its beginning brought about the spirit of charity. It brought respect to the first believers. Even their enemies admired their selflessness towards their neighbors, and the care with which they met their neighbors' needs. As the centuries passed, glorious memories of their beneficial actions in

---

12   The author attributes this to J. J. Rousseau, *Pensamientos*, p. 3, but it is unclear what book this is.
13   2 Cor. 7.

aid of every class of victims of misfortune were left in every region. Oh, what a beautiful chain of benefactions were offered to us by Christian charity in the Christian centuries! She founded institutes for men and women who consecrated themselves to serving and helping their neighbors in whatever ways that could be useful and according to whatever forms misfortune took. They built palaces everywhere to receive the sick, orphaned, children abandoned by heartless mothers, sick old people, the weak, the poor, pilgrims, and repentant women. They were not satisfied with only keeping the doors of these palaces open to the unfortunate that they received. They went out, and sought out the unfortunate in their own sad homes. They came to them as if incognito, either to aid the poor who were ashamed, to help families in need, or to alleviate other hidden human miseries.

Only the Catholic religion produced these generous women who got into the middle of those living in great misery to bring aid to them, and whose self-denial elicited the following words from the patriarch of modern impiety: "Perhaps there is on earth nothing greater than the sacrifice of beauty, of youth, and sometimes of elevated birth that the delicate sex brought to console and aid this multitude of human miseries in the hospitals. The mere sight of them humbled the proud, and is so repugnant to our nature." These women appeared so elevated, but the Mercedarians or the Trinitarians looked no less high. They redeemed captives by giving themselves as captives in stinking prisons, or were forced to take on extremely distressing work. No fewer were the martyrs who shed their blood to lavish their goodness on their fellows. There were also many heroes who sought salvation in places that had the smell of death. They ended up in the grave in the springtime of their lives, perhaps with no other witness to their heroism than God to whom they had surrendered their beautiful souls. There is no religion that expresses such beauty, tenderness, and charm. Nor is there any such institution that so beautifully and positively supports victims of pain or misfortune.

V

If the faith instructs men, improves customs, and aids misfortune, we can infer, as a legitimate consequence, that its most beneficial influence is on society, since society consists of men. Actually, historical events that came to appear around the nineteenth century reflected this generosity that was favorable to societies.

Whether the enemies of our holy religion like it or not, it will always be a fact, and a public fact properly proven by history, that it made shameful vices, cruel sacrifices, and barbaric customs of pagan society disappear. Softening customs and inspiring beautiful virtues, it formed a new society entirely distinct from the old one. The new one outlawed the exposure and death of the newly born, bloody human sacrifices, the rights of the stronger over slaves, the vilification of women, and other such excesses.

Despite impiety, facts no less certain and enlightening show that the Catholic faith later opposed the rage of the northern hordes and even formed civilized nations out of them. The faith demolished the power of the Crescent in many countries, freeing many there of the slavery and barbarism to which they had been reduced. It extended its generosity beyond the seas, forming thousands of civilized peoples out of the same number of savage peoples. It always opposed the excesses of sects that appeared throughout the centuries, sometimes preventing disasters that threatened the peoples, and other times remedying the destruction that they caused. Finally, it promoted good customs, science, the arts, industry, and work everywhere.

It left much testimony that attested to this, including in masterly writings that addressed all branches of human knowledge; in incomparable poetic productions; in paintings that served as models; in architectural monuments of the first order; in the most moving and elevated pieces of music; in the best materials of every kind; and in agriculture. These facts, one brighter than the next, spoke at such heights about our religion, and did not fail to confess even to many of these same enemies that they could understand that to deny this would be to give sufficient motive to qualify them either as ignorant of historical events or as men marked by bad faith.

What the Catholic religion did for society in its initial appearance in the world and in the course of centuries, it is still doing today through its teachings, doctrines, and multitude of beneficial institutions. These institutions have been created and maintained by its spirit. The goods of every kind that this religion brings forth will undoubtedly continue to be produced in the future because it has the same resources now that it always had. It is certain that it will never lack these. It is the only institution that possesses adequate means to unite men with the closest bonds. Only it has the precepts that provide the best foundation for society. It teaches that all authority stems from God. This teaching makes its public authority more respectable and gives it inexpressible power because it is a duty of conscience to obey it.

But at the same time, it teaches public authority that it cannot abuse its power because this power has been given it only for the good of subordinates. This includes promoting the good, chastising rebels, persecuting vice, encouraging virtue, and working toward justice. Religion calls for reciprocal obligations between those who command and those who obey; between the great and the small; between the rich and the poor; among all the various social classes. The fulfillment of these obligations is necessary for the most charming harmony and the sweetest peace among everyone.

Religion is equipped, moreover, with another admirable means for uniting men. This is the strong and mysterious bond of charity. This patient, benign, and humble charity is empty of egoism or competition. It condemns all anger, envy, and aversion. It can bring about the great idea of unity that propelled Our Savior Jesus Christ to institute the Church and to implore the Eternal Father in the tenderest way in solemn moments.[14] The first Christians achieved this great principle of unity because they observed the teachings of the gospel. Among them reigned only the same thought, desire, and love. Having handed their souls over to God, they were like one soul. Their hearts, all beating to the yearning for the same charity, formed a single heart.[15] There is nothing so admirable as the gentle and right laws of the gospel. Nothing is so effective as these laws are for uniting men of various social classes and even of different countries. These laws establish among them concord, peace, and harmony while rooting out all division, strife, and fighting.

True civilization is found only where Catholic belief unites and strengthens social bonds; where truth and virtue reign, and error and vice are exiled; where religion encourages love for friendship, the family, and the fatherland; and where every social movement turns on the indestructible axis of the great principle of faith. This faith even supports modern societies, despite the war that these societies wage against it. This faith, even today, is the strong and robust dam that contains anarchy's destructive waves. This faith, with luck, animates the great masses. With the teachings that it gives, the

14   John 17:22.
15   Acts 4:32.

virtues that it inspires, and the obedience of the authorities that it preaches, this faith prevents the empire of evil from dominating everything. Yes, she still nourishes the working classes with the Catholic spirit. She still lives from the faith. She still leads from her principles. All of these characteristics save societies and demonstrate her beneficial influence over them.

May we also know, my children, how to value this precious gift of faith, that the Lord in his great mercy granted us, along with so many goods for both the individual and for society. Let us not be ungrateful for this great gift from God, and let us remain faithful to our belief, which is the only one, and to persevere in the teachings of Jesus Christ. Let us become stronger in the faith, and grow more and more in it *through acts of thanksgiving*, as the apostle said. Let us strive above all to work in harmony with the teachings of the faith. This is the best way to give thanks to our Lord Jesus Christ for this favor, and the best way to participate in the goods that it provides. You are so fortunate, my children, because you still have faith, but you will be more fortunate if you know how to conserve it! With this in mind, we move on to sound the alert that you be vigilant and do not let yourselves be seduced by preachers of a false philosophy that is contrary to the teachings of Jesus Christ. This philosophy only brings misfortune, blood, and desolation.

VI

The alert is sounded when a danger threatens us, with the goal that this can be averted and no one perishes. Is our faith threatened at this time? Unfortunately, I must say yes, and even add that the danger is great because there are so many enemies fighting us. They are determined in their undertaking of tearing the peoples and nations away from the bosom of the Church. The sacred Vatican Council denounced this danger. It declared, "No one is unaware that the heresies banned by the Fathers of Trent have slowly split into many separate sects. They fight among themselves in such a way that many have lost their faith in Jesus Christ. They no longer hold the Bible as sacred though they had previously affirmed it to be the sole origin and judge of Christian doctrine. They have instead associated it with mythical fables. Then the doctrine of rationalism or naturalism was born and began to spread over the entire globe. It attacked the Christian religion by every means because it is a supernatural institution. It strove with great passion to establish the reign of what it calls *pure reason* and *nature*. This excludes human intelligence and the life and customs of the peoples of Christ, who is our sole Lord and Savior. After abandoning and rejecting the Christian religion and denying God and his Christ, the spirit of many people yielded to the abyss of pantheism, naturalism, and atheism. They did this to the point of denying the same rational nature and all the rules of righteousness and justice. They instead strove to destroy the primary foundations of human society. It happened that, having extended this impiety everywhere, even many children of the Catholic Church became separated from true piety. By the gradual abandonment of truths, their Catholic sense became lukewarm. Misled by many alien teachings, and badly confusing nature and grace, human science and divine faith, they sought to alter the true sense of the dogmas that are believed and taught by the holy mother Church, and to corrupt and put in danger the authenticity and integrity of the faith."[16]

My children, this is the danger denounced by our holy mother Church which was united in an ecumenical council. We therefore cannot doubt the existence of this

---

16   Dogmatic Constitution *Dei Filius* (Brian Welter translation from Moreno's Spanish).

danger that threatens our faith. We must be vigilant and on notice so that we are not seduced and destroyed by this danger. The enemies of our faith make seductive promises of bliss and prosperity once we abandon the faith and follow their doctrines, but a years-long and painful experience demonstrates that the enemies are not only incapable of fulfilling these promises, but produce effects that are entirely the opposite. These effects plunge peoples into revolutions, fatal anarchy, and ruin.

VII

The Catholic faith has always had enemies. In every epoch, they appeared and waged harsh wars against it. In every era, errors attacked the Church. Supporters of these errors drew on all sorts of means, even from those who had rejected natural decency. But now in our days, we see a multitude of men animated by a systematic hate against Catholic belief that they cannot hide. They have decided to ban the church's teachings in the government of the people, to regulate society without its dogmas and precepts, and to bring them to complete forgetfulness. We hear everywhere the voices of these men who are infatuated with a vain enlightenment. These masters are sons of the father of lies and emissaries of the angel of *non serviam*. They promise the people happiness and good fortune, but with the indispensable condition that they leave the faith, abandon Catholic beliefs, and adore the idols of reason and human liberty that they present. Full of pride, they present themselves to men as the only ones capable of giving them enlightenment, advancement, wealth, happiness, and every other kind of good. They say this all in circles and gatherings with seductive language such as artificial phrases picked up from streets and plazas. They spread this through books, leaflets, and newspapers, and with astonishing activity that is worthy of a great cause.

Be on notice, my children, according to the counsel of the apostle, so that you are not seduced by these men with promises that they cannot and will not be able to keep. They base their promises on principles that disregard God, who is the source and origin of all blessings, peace, advancement, and good. The facts, which must be the most valuable proof for these men and their positivism, speak in a most convincing way. We can come to the facts to see the fruits that these doctrines have produced. They are contrary to the teachings of Catholicism.

We do not have to go back far in history to see the achievements of these men who disregard the doctrines of the Catholic faith in order to govern the people. They assure that human reason is all we need to provide goods of every kind. In the past century, they gave us convincing, if terrible, proof. They acclaimed reason as a god. They erected altars. They accorded her a public cult, and went on triumphal processions with her. They adored her with unspeakable enthusiasm and unheard of delirium. Reason, or support for reason, was legislated and brought into work and government. Absolutes regarding God and the doctrines that were revealed to men in order to conduct them to their immortal destinies were dispensed with. If reason could have made the people happy, it would have done better at this point than ever before because it governed without hindrance or the smallest obstacle. It reigned with full powers. Did it thereby provide this much vaunted happiness? Let the facts speak for us: They speak of so many innocent victims who were sacrificed, so much blood spilled, so much misfortune and destruction, so much crime and horror that distinguish this epoch and mark it as one of the most terrifying and ominous of humanity.

These same appalling scenes have been reproduced, in small and large scales, wherever the government of the people preferred to exclude the Catholic faith and disregard its saving doctrines. There can be no other result. Those who prepare the way to remove the faith from the bosom of societies, as if it is a hindrance, as they say, to modern progress, an obstacle to the progress of civilization, an outdated thing that is incapable of providing any good to the people, can do nothing but deprive man of all sweet and noble satisfaction and prevent him from aspiring to every sublime and elevated aspiration. They make men numb to every great and generous sentiment. They fill their spirits with discontent and sadness. They equate them to animals, and destroy their bliss with the satisfaction of carnal appetites. They end restraint on all their passions. They bring misery upon them and provoke them to commit every class of crime.

Yes, men who before suffered setbacks in this life with sweet Christian resignation, who endured their misfortunes with the consoling hope of eternal reward, who in their misery and hardships raised their eyes heavenward and imagined this blissful future, are today victims of horrible skepticism. They are without this Christian resignation, without hopes, without the comfort of this happy and bright future. They cannot experience anything other than weariness, anguish, restlessness, and desperation. Given that they have nothing more to aspire to than the joys of this life, if they do not have this, the logical consequence is that they search for these joys at any price and in every way, even criminal ways. This leads to appalling revolutions, bloody battles, and social troubles which include communism, nihilism, anarchism, and the use of dynamite. This sad and terrifying spectacle that promotes modern liberties everywhere frightens the very same people who established these principles that have such fatal consequences.

VIII

Doctrines that deify human reason and make it supreme over good, bad, and everything else, drive away revealed religion and deny the rights of God while proclaiming those of humans. These doctrines teach how to live entirely independently of all divine and human laws. But they can give no other fruits than those expressed. Those who spread this teaching try to conceal the absurd and horrible aspects of these doctrines with the pompous names of liberty, equality, fraternity, illumination, progress, and so on. But the facts have clearly shown that the word *liberty* only signifies corruption of customs. *Equality* is the negation of all authority; that *fraternity* spilled torrents of human blood. *Illumination* does not mean God, religion, conscience, any duty, or any sense of shame. *Progress* means to become equal to animals, without thought of anything else except how to multiply pleasures, find every happiness in material life, and dismiss all notions of spirituality. Still — oh, such pain! — to state that appearances deceived and seduced so many, that as St. Jerome said in his time that all the world found Arianism without knowing it, in the same way we can say today that the world is in the grip of modern liberties almost without knowing about these, if one exempts men who are blessed to have unconditionally followed the teachings of the Church, the Teacher of the truth.

I warn you, my children! Be on the alert that these men, with their false promises, do not seduce you, because experience teaches us so often the object that they strive for and all that they can give with their false philosophy and doctrines that do not conform to the doctrines of Jesus Christ our Divine Savior. With Christian courage, reject their exposed teachings, laid bare in conversations, discourses, and the multitude of corrupting books, revolutionary leaflets, and furious periodicals. There are echoes of impiety and anarchism, and elements of death for individuals and people who are demoralized, degraded, and debased by them. Don't forget the harsh lessons of the past, and take from them what is useful for the future. The people are more or less happy according to their greater or lesser practice of Catholicism. And wherever these teachings are not taken into account, human reason dominates and the faith is forgotten. Then disbelief reigns and the rule of Jesus Christ is not recognized. Nothing more can be hoped for than what is already seen, which is horrible torment, dreadful unrest, social misfortune, and death and desolation.

IX

In His sublime plan, the Lord has chosen us to be the first watchmen in this beloved diocese, and for this we give the sound of alarm, a sound that we hope is repeated for these sentinels who occupy the advanced positions in the safekeeping of the people of God. Beloved priests, our co-workers, especially you parish priests, you are the sentinels who should be keeping an eye on the Christian people to whom you are entrusted day and night so that the enemies do not authorize the faithful and snatch them away from the beautiful city of God, the sole place which has bliss, peace, and happiness, and take them as captives to the horrible city of the devil, where everything is disorder, horror, and confusion. Work like good laborers in the vineyard of the Great Father of the family, pulling up the weeds of error and vice so that abundant fruit, virtue, and good works are harvested. Pray frequently, offer sacrifices, and humbly ask God for the mercy that he does not take back from us the great gift of faith, and that he does not permit the great misfortunes that others experience to come to our people. Strive to turn the hearts of youth towards the clerical state, and take care that those who enter the seminary have a love of piety and the things of God, so that someone can help you in your ministry and can fill your position when the Lord calls you to receive the reward for your work.

The first object of our attention will be the seminary. We will strive to make it into a true seedbed, not only of scholars, but principally of saints and zealous priests. We will help the intelligent and virtuous superiors that direct it with all of our powers. They inspire the most absolute confidence in us. They have always inspired us in everything that relates to the service of God and His great glory. Help us, therefore, beloved parish priests, in this great work, as you do in other areas of your ministry. We hope much from you, because we assume that you are filled with the Spirit of God and hope to work for your own sanctity and those of your neighbors. Meanwhile, know that you occupy a special place in our heart, and that we will always be willing to hear you, help you, and share with you the work and effort.

We expect no less from the priests who live united according to the spirit of the zealous Philip Neri,[17] as well as the religious communities, because we have ample motives to support this consoling hope. We find ourselves in the position to appreciate the great services that Our Divine Redeemer Jesus Christ provides to the Church. We know you, we appreciate you, we love you, tireless workers. As I greet you with our overflowing heart, we offer you, with the greatest pleasure, the most decisive support and firmest assistance. I hope you multiply like the stars in the firmament! What greater happiness would there be for us than to see ourselves surrounded by numerous workers who help us not only to sustain the faith of those

---

17   By this, Moreno is referring to the Oratorians of Pasto [German translator's note].

who possess the inexpressible joy to live in it, but also to spread and take it to those who have not been illuminated with its brilliant light, but who still find themselves in the shadows of death? Spread out to the regions of Caquetá! Unfortunate disbelievers who live there and roam around! You are in my memory, and I will not forget you!

We also need, in a special way, the help of prayer, of intercession of God our Lord, so that we can illuminate the world with his divine light, and help ourselves with his powerful grace for the good performance of our thorny and heavy responsibility. Who can provide us with this invaluable good better than you, who live exclusively for him? You are the brides of the Immaculate Lamb. You are his because of your religious vows. Live exclusively for him. You can call him Spouse and have the closest connection to him, and he will hear you when you call out for help to him as your pastor. Do this therefore in the security that you will be receiving our prayers, paternal affection, and special care for your great advancement in every way.

We also turn in a special way to the people who are dedicated to the teaching of various grades, and we commission you with the precious blood of Our Divine Redeemer, that you form the minds and hearts of youth in everything according to the teachings of our holy, catholic, Roman, and apostolic religion, because only by doing that do you demonstrate fidelity to your mission and make yourselves well-deserving of religion and country. You can do much, beloved teachers, for the good of souls, religion, and society by inculcating love for the truth of Catholic belief and for the Christian virtues in your students, distance from vice, and aversion to all belief that is contrary to Catholic teaching. This is the only thing that can perfect man, make him useful to society, and lead him to the achievement of his true destiny.

Lastly, we hope of all the faithful entrusted to our care that they help us in our duty of leading them to the paths of eternal salvation, filling each of them with their respective duties and leading a truly Christian life, as they are and show themselves in every circumstance to always be faithful sons of our holy mother, the Catholic Church. They think in all matters as she thinks, accepts only what she accepts, rejects what she rejects, and condemns what she condemns, whether in speculative truths that they must believe, or in practical truths which aim to direct and mend our actions. So that you can better fulfill these duties, we recommend that you enter or enlist in a pious association that prescribes frequent reception of the sacraments. These are a powerful means of developing piety and wonderful stimuli for the practice of good works which cannot be practiced in another way.

X

Great, so very great, is our joy in knowing that the diocese we have come to direct has already been consecrated to the Divine Heart of Jesus, and that the apostolate of prayer has already spread. Given that our bishop coat of arms is the Heart of Jesus and will remain so, and that we bear witness to this same coat of arms as we confess that this sweet and loving Heart is our strength and our refuge, our soul cannot but overflow with contentment and happiness in the knowledge that our new flock professes their devotion and worship. How could it be otherwise? How could we not feel the greatest satisfaction to see that the Sacred Heart of Jesus is worshiped after the great Pius IX declared, and the wise Leo XIII repeated, that devotion to the Sacred Heart of Jesus will be the salvation of the world, and that it is the remedy for the great evils that modern societies suffer? Who cannot see, in fact, in this Divine Heart the remedy for the evils that the current world suffers? Gentle and humble, it condemns the spirit of arrogance and pride. It is obedient to the Heavenly Father until death, teaches submission to superiors, and destroys the spirit of independence. It is pacific until the extreme, like the bent over reed that does not break, and inspires the sweetest peace. With its crown of thorns and its cross, it teaches and preaches mortification. It condemns this burning thirst for material pleasures that devours modern people. It burns with the flames of charity and unreservedly gives Itself to men. Excited by mutual love, it calls for everyone to be united without mutual distrust, divisions, or fights, like true brothers, all sons of the same Father who is in Heaven, who are called to enjoy the same inheritance.

This advantageous and beautiful union strives to achieve the devotion of the apostolate of prayer because it unites the Heart of Jesus with the prayers, sacrifices, the suffering, and all the good works, intentions, emotions, and hearts of the faithful. They do not have to think of or want anything else but what the Sacred Heart thinks and wants. This is the glory of the Celestial Father and the salvation of all men. This devotion is not a hindrance for the other devotions, but can instead be a mysterious bond that unites everyone, giving everyone greater splendor and making the other devotions more acceptable to the Divine Majesty. They become more purified through the holy intentions of the Sacred Heart of Jesus, and are united to his infinite merits. We therefore recommend to everyone a great increase in this devotion. We request that this enable the practice of the sweet and full joys of communion of reparation. This reparation gives so much good to the souls that do this, and so much consolation to the Sacred Heart of Jesus. It is insulted in so many ways by the enemies of the Sacrament of his love, and with the persecution that is done against his Holy Church, to his Vicar on Earth, the Holy Pontiff in Rome, to his priests and to all those who are associated with him. I pray, my sons, that the Sacred Heart of Jesus reigns in our souls! That it reigns in families! That it reigns among the people! That it reigns in society and that everyone will be saved! Salvation is not possible outside of him.

Love also with all your heart, and pay homage to the tender and related worship of Mary, the Most Holy, the exalted Mother of God and our tender Mother, because it is known that no grace flows from heaven to earth that does not pass through her blessed hands, according to the teaching of St. Bernard.[18]

The devotion to the glorious patriarch St. Joseph, eminent head of the Sacred Family and patron of the whole Church, is inseparable from these devotions. Our Lord Jesus Christ wanted his father to be honored in these times as never before, and he is pleased to pour out rich graces on those who invoke his powerful patronage, and to multiply miracles in favor of those who honor him.

Let us conclude, my sons, by remembering that our sole business that is truly important here on earth is, as the Catechism states, *to serve and love God, so that later on we can possess him and enjoy him in heaven.* This is our goal. All our efforts must direct us to its accomplishment. If we achieve this, we have achieved everything. If we lose it, we have lost everything. Let us not value the things of the world more than they merit. We must give to the things of heaven their due importance, as they are the only truly necessary things. The things of the earth come to their end, as they pass through and then disappear in a short time, while the things of heaven are eternal. Let us aspire to eternal things. Let us constantly sigh for our heavenly home. Let us work to attain the inexpressible delights that are reserved there for us if

18   Serm. III in vig. Nat. Dom.

we are victorious in the battles of this life. That you pledge yourselves to this future heavenly happiness, we give to all this blessing that comes with the most loving greeting in the name of the Father ✠ and the Son ✠ and the Holy Spirit ✠. Amen.

Given in our episcopal palace of Pasto, on the Feast of the Sacred Heart of Jesus, June 12, 1896.
✠ Fr. Ezequiel, Bishop of Pasto.
Sent by Reverend Anselmo Guerrero, Secretary.

FOURTH
Pastoral Letter

DIRECTED TO THE CLERGY AND
FAITHFUL OF THE DIOCESE OF PASTO
ON THE OCCASION OF LENT, 1897.
HIS EXCELLENCY POINTS OUT SOME
OF THE PRINCIPAL ACTIONS TO
PUT INTO PRACTICE SO THAT THE
PRECIOUS GIFT OF FAITH IS NOT LOST.

To the honored clergy and the faithful of our diocese:
Greetings and peace in Our Lord Jesus Christ.

WE ARE AT PRESENT SO CLOSE to Lent, which is the greatest of all things that are called holy not only because of the august mysteries that are commemorated and celebrated by our holy mother Church in this time, but also because in this time we must attend in a special way to sanctifying the soul and doing whatever is possible to bring about its eternal salvation. We can do no less than to invite you to fulfill the intentions and high view of our holy mother. Try to pass this time in a manner that is responsive to her loving concern. This includes works of piety, exercises of penitence, meditation on what it cost Our Lord Jesus Christ to liberate us from eternal death, and the consideration that the sole necessary truth for us is to serve and love God in this life. If we do this all, afterwards we can see, possess, and enjoy him in eternity. This is our goal. It is for this that the Lord created us.

Our Lord Jesus Christ suffered and died so that we can reach this high and sublime destiny. We must strive for him and, galvanizing ourselves with all our forces, overcome with valor all the obstacles that stand in the way against its achievement. The other way will lead us to lose this happy goal and fall into eternal misfortune.

It is the faith that teaches us these great truths that we have just expressed. This same faith tells us that in this important issue of the achievement of our ultimate end, in other words, of the salvation of our souls, there is only one way for all time. When our soul is lost, it cannot be recovered. If this is what the faith teaches us, why don't men give the due weight to these great questions, the only ones that are truly necessary? Ah! It is because, unfortunately, there is so little faith on earth. Some have gone so far as to say that either we have already entered the calamitous end times, or in the least that these are very close. Jesus Christ Our Lord mentioned this time when he said to his apostles, "But yet the Son of man, when he cometh, shall he find, think you, faith on earth?"[1] Whatever things may be, there is no doubt that there is much lack of faith among men. Who does not see everywhere today many men who boast in being known for the names of errors opposed to Catholic doctrine? Some call themselves atheists, others deists, still others pantheists. There are materialists, rationalists, and many masons. All of them—and many more—call themselves liberals. This is the common name for all modern errors, because these errors all found friendly reception within liberalism. As well, how many of those who call themselves Catholic have an intact faith with all the qualities necessary for salvation? Oh, so many errors, so much deceit, and so much sin against the faith are found even in many of the people who say that they believe! There is no doubt

---

1   Luke 18:8.

that there is everywhere an atmosphere of disbelief and indifference towards religion and the death of the soul. The fatal influence of this disbelief and indifference will make us all feel this death if we don't take the necessary precautions. We believe that there is a pressing need to look out for contagion of this heretical epidemic that surrounds us. For this reason, instead of another matter that could be dealt with in this pastoral letter, we have decided to stress some of the principal means that we must put into practice in order not to lose the precious and inestimable gift of faith that the Lord, in his mercy, has granted us. We are convinced that we will accomplish a great deed for the souls that receive our teaching with obedience and the desire for spiritual development, because the Lord is not lacking in grace when souls find themselves in a good disposition.

According to the Council of Trent, "Belief is the beginning, the foundation, and the root of justification" (Session 6, Chapter 8). It is necessary to maintain this because, without this, we would be striving in vain to establish the beautiful edifice of Christian sanctity, to please God, and to attain eternal salvation. The Lord our God, with his conduct, teaches us of the great necessity to guard faith with special care. God has sheltered, or let us say, has surrounded this virtue with an impregnable wall that he has instituted with beautiful care. One single mortal sin is enough to bring death to this love, and killing this, the soul also dies. But this very sin, that kills this love and the soul, cannot get to this faith that remains and subsists in the soul even though it is dead. It is the principle with which the grace of God can resuscitate it, and the root from which, with the same divine grace, the leafy tree of Christian holiness can once again sprout.

Concluding from this preceding doctrine, no matter how many or horrible a man's sins are, if he conserves the faith, his conversion to God is not so difficult. But if he comes to lose his faith, this is the most difficult thing because he lacks the foundation of the edifice which can be built on, and the roots that bring up the sap that gives life to his soul, which is dead due to sin. See, then, that it is of the greatest importance to know and put into practice the means of conserving the faith and avoiding the dangers that lead to its loss.

The first way to conserve the faith *is a humble obedience to the guidelines of our Holy Mother the Church.* The good Catholic humbly accepts and believes everything that the Holy Church orders and teaches. Suspicious of his own judgment, he eagerly follows even the smallest rules of the Holy See, whether these are doctrinal, discipline-related, or other. He desires to subject his weak intelligence to every implication of what he believes to be the Master of truth, and to see things, and to judge, believe, and feel them as how the Master sees, judges, feels, and proposes them. What appears to the Church as good and true appears also to him that way. Far from feeling mistrust, he feels joyful in thinking that he cannot be deluded by something that is directed by the Holy Spirit and is supported by the infallible promises of its divine Founder, Jesus Christ, our Lord. Whoever thinks and acts in this way will conserve his faith because this consists of the absolute submission of understanding to God's authority. Whoever submits even in the smallest things is far from lacking submission in the graver things. Not only this, but also the faithful who let themselves be governed in everything by the rules of the Church achieve what the Vatican Council calls the *sensus catholicus.* This consists of a supernatural disposition for promptly and safely discerning truth from error. These believers see themselves strongly driven by the truth that they love and savor even while feeling profound aversion for error. Simple faithful, gifted with this Catholic sense, saw certain errors with more clarity, and described them with more precision, than prominent men who lacked this sense. In giving humble obedience to the discernment of our Holy Mother Church, those who are far from losing their faith can see things easily.

Pride, in contrast, is the origin of all heresies because it leads to rebellion against God and his Church and proclaims the independence of its own reason. God, though, resists the proud and gives grace to the humble.[2] Jesus therefore said in the most expressive and tender way: "I confess to thee, O Father, Lord of heaven and earth, because thou hast hid these things from the wise and prudent, and hast revealed them to the little ones."[3] God illuminates the humble with his light so that they can see the truths of salvation with clarity, and permits that those who boast of wisdom remain without this light. The mysteries of the faith do not radiate light for those who rebel against the authority of God. In their misfortune, they seem to receive more light from reading Aristotle or Plato than from reading sacred Scripture. Pride blinds them, and so they only see the vice put in front of them. That vice is always the non-subordination of their understanding, their will, and other things that belong to them because pride cannot endure any superiority. *Non serviam.* I will not serve, said the proud angel Lucifer. And I will not serve, repeat all of his minions, from the most extreme atheist to the most moderate liberal, declaring with their snooty voices their rebellion against God, who must be obeyed by everyone as the Master and Lord of all. "That man, by a necessity of his nature, is wholly subject to the most faithful and ever-enduring power of God; and that, as a consequence, any liberty, except that which consists in submission to God and

2   1 Pet. 5:5.
3   Matt. 11:25.

in subjection to his will, is unintelligible. To deny the existence of this authority in God, or to refuse to submit to it, means to act, not as a free man, but as the rebel who abuses his freedom; and in such a disposition of mind the capital and deadly vice of liberalism essentially consists."[4] Humble obedience to the discernment of our Holy Mother Church is the way, my children, to keep the faith, and to avoid falling into the widespread errors, through misfortune, of our time, which are the chief reason for the rebellion that is caused by pride.

The second way to keep the faith *is a truly Christian life*. Our Lord Jesus Christ said that he came into the world so that we could have life—and abundant life. To secure it in this way, there is no doubt that we can have Christian life in abundance. As the faith is the foundation of this life, there is no doubt that, having abundance in Christian life, we also have an abundance of faith.

The Divine Savior left abundant resources so that we could have the abundance of life that he came to bring us, and he has the desire that we have it. His examples, teachings, divine preaching, and, above all, sacraments, are admirable means of giving us spiritual life and life in abundance. Whoever avails himself of these ways will live the life of faith and grace, true life that we see in everyone who duly follows religious practices, attentively listens to the divine word, reflects on the examples and teachings of Jesus Christ, and receives the sacraments. These works of piety conserve and build up the light of the faith, and even bring about a such a great liveliness that with this, those who have it penetrate somehow the invisible, and see the eternal truths and mysteries in a transparent manner, which is unknown to those who do not take advantage of these ways given by Jesus Christ so that we can have an abundance of spiritual life.

4   Pope Leo XIII, 1888, *Libertas*.

54

Through religious practices, we remember, serve, and love God. But if we stop that, the love of God slowly weakens, and the light of faith goes out. Lack of faith is the consequence of forgetting God. This comes about when we abandon religious duties and practices of piety. Forgetfulness of God is followed by the life of sin. Those who enter into sin easily come to lose faith because the existence of the truths that the faith teaches are awkward for them. Faith, cause for joy and happiness for the just man, is cause for anxiety and fear for the sinner. This explains why the just man always grows in faith, while the sinner tends to not believe, wavers, doubts, and ends by totally losing faith. Yes, the faith makes the most consoling promises to the just. It shows him a happy future. Faith offers him inexpressible and eternal bliss. Feeling this way, he not only has no motive to rid himself of the truths of the faith, but in fact holds them and increases them in the ardent desire for the fulfillment of these truths. He already feels in his faithful practice a foreshadowed joy, which is the prelude to the hoped-for eternity. The total opposite happens to men who are given to sinful pleasures that are prohibited by God. The faith places them in front of the strict judges of God, lets them hear the terrible sentences of condemnation, and shows them the eternity of the pains of hell. All of that is so unpleasant, bitter, and terrible. They therefore try to drive out these thoughts that do not allow them to feel joy from the pleasures of life. They strive to believe in nothing, and conclude by saying that they don't believe. They even mock and deride the most sacred and saintly things. These men do not like it that God and punishment exist, just like an evildoer dislikes it that there are judges and prisons. This prompts their decision to deny these truths.

It frequently happens that error leads to corruption of customs. But more frequently, especially among

Christians, the corruption of customs leads to error or the loss of faith. St. Cyprian says, "No one believes that the good can abandon the Church. The wind carries away the straw and chaff, but not the grains." Church history provides us with many examples that confirm this truth. We can say that the corruption of customs has created more apostates from the faith than the persecution and torments of tyrants. Masses of people and entire nations abandoned the faith because they had already been prepared by the corruption of customs. The enemies of the Catholic Church know this well, and, to this end, their battle plan is to corrupt. Pius IX on May 29, 1876, stated, "Their first thought was to corrupt the spirit and heart of the people, and mainly of youth." An official document of the leadership of the secret society states: "Let us never tire of corrupting. It is decided in our discussions that we do not want more Christians. Let us therefore popularize vice among the masses. They can sense it with their five senses, and swallow it and be saturated in it. If their hearts are corrupted, there will be no more Catholics."

A truly Christian life is one that can save us from the loss of faith and from apostasy while in the middle of such danger. Let us live in such a way that we will always be in a state of wanting there to be God, an immortal soul, a future life with rewards and punishments, and, in a word, the certainty that everything that our Holy Mother Church teaches us is true. Let us follow the counsel of the apostle who says, "Having faith and a good conscience, which some rejecting have made shipwreck concerning the faith."[5]

The third way that we note for conserving the faith is to flee *as much as possible from all communication with those who profess doctrines that are contrary to*

---

5   1 Tim. 1:19.

Catholicism. Interacting with these men puts us in danger of losing faith. It is necessary to avoid them.

St. Paul the apostle wrote to Timothy, "Now these avoid. For of these sort . . . resist the truth, men corrupted in mind, reprobate concerning the faith."[6] In the same letter, he states that the talk of these men eats away at things like cancer.[7] And Cornelius à Lapide, commenting on these words, declares, "All the Holy Fathers taught that we must flee heretics like the plague." Our holy mother the Church also teaches us to keep a distance from them with her conduct and way of proceeding with those who lack faith.

These teachings from God himself, written down in Holy Scripture, and those of the Church and the Holy Fathers, should be enough for all good Catholics so they can understand the danger of losing the faith when they interact with those who do not follow the Church's thinking and the obligation to avoid dealing with them when possible. What other authorities desire that we take note of and teach this duty? None other, nor could there be any other worth more and deserving of more credit, because God is the truth itself, and cannot deceive himself or us.

Let us add that reason and experience also demonstrate this danger and, consequently, the obligation to avoid it. Interaction with other men exercises in us such an influence that we slowly become like them. Hence the adage, "Tell me who you hang out with, and I'll tell you who you are." When we spend time with someone, we imperceptibly take on his way of being. We make his thoughts ours. We come to feel like he does, lament the things he laments, feel joy for the things he feels joy for, applaud what he applauds, and condemn what he condemns. We are, in a word, what he is, or at least the perfect image.

6   2 Tim. 3:5–8.
7   2 Tim. 2:17.

At the beginning, perhaps one does not approve of his evil insinuations, and even expresses disgust. But bit by bit, this disgust disappears, and then these are not even thought of as evil. Later, they are regarded as humorous events. Finally, they penetrate the entire soul, and come to occupy the same place that religious beliefs used to occupy. This process converts the man into an unbeliever, an impious person. Oh, how many have had what we have just described shamefully happen to them! How many have lost their faith from interacting with those who mock them! How many have even lost their soul, their poor soul, and for all of eternity, from dealing with unbelievers? One single unbeliever is enough to bring about the loss of many who interact with him. This is seen everywhere, in all times, and even today.

We said when we began to discuss this point that we must flee from communication with those people who profess doctrines that are contrary to Catholicism. Consequently, liberals of every shade are included in this because the Pope has condemned liberalism in all its varieties as an error, that is, in every one of its principles, and even in its latest and hypocritical bluff of *Catholic liberalism*. That is why it is necessary to avoid liberals as much as possible. We not only have to flee interaction with liberals who declare themselves atheists, materialists, rationalists, masons, etc. Much more so, we also have to flee liberal Catholics because they are the most dangerous. They do the most damage to the Church and to souls. In a letter on March 6, 1873, Pius IX said,

> Though the children of this world be wiser than the children of light, their snares and their violence would undoubtedly have less success if a great number of those who call themselves Catholics did not extend a friendly hand to them.

Yes, unfortunately, there are those who seem to want to walk in agreement with our enemies and try to build an alliance between light and darkness and an accord between justice and iniquity, by means of those so-called liberal Catholic doctrines. These doctrines, based on the most pernicious principles, adulate the civil power when it invades the spiritual arena and urges souls to respect or at least tolerate the most iniquitous laws, as if it had not been written absolutely that no one can serve two masters.

They are certainly much more dangerous and more baneful than our declared enemies. They not only support their efforts, perhaps without realizing it, but also maintain themselves at the very edge of condemned opinions. They take on an appearance of integrity and sound doctrine. They beguile unwise lovers of reconciliation and deceive the honest, who would revolt against open error. In this way, they divide the minds, destroy unity, and weaken the forces that should be assembled against the enemy.[8]

So says the Pope, as cited. As you can see, such a clear, conclusive, and expressive document needs no comment. One must flee from interaction with liberal Catholics much more than with the open enemies of religion, because the former are *more dangerous and more false. They drag souls away for submission, or at least tolerate the most evil laws.*

We cannot pass over another, more important, warning on this point which we are discussing. It is the following: directors of Catholic associations must take special care

---

8   Pope Pius IX, Letter to the president and members of the Saint Ambrose Circle of Milan, March 6, 1873, in *I Papi e la Gioventù*, (Rome: Editrice A. V. E., 1944). https://tfpstudentaction. org/resources/forgotten-truths/no-one-can-serve-two-masters-1

to block access to their associations to people who do not think in all ways like our Holy Mother the Church does. We must not forget that the mason uses every means to make war against the Church. In Brazil, the masons have come to dominate the guilds and fraternities to such a degree that, in view of the danger, Pius IX called this to the attention of the bishops and ordered the suppression of these brotherhoods. The same must be done with liberals. Directors of Catholic associations must exclude not only extreme liberals from the association, but also those who strive to reconcile Catholicism with liberalism, that is, Catholic liberals. One needs to say to them, with Pius IX, that *it is not possible to serve two masters.*

Here it would also be appropriate to declare that, as another way to conserve the faith, we must avoid reading harmful books, leaflets, and newspapers. We already addressed this point in our pastoral letter of August 10 of last year. No one should think himself so firm in the faith that he has nothing to fear from those who have no faith. Even with his extraordinary wisdom from God, Solomon bent his knee before idols due to his close interactions with idolatrous women. This frightening example, like many others, should make us distrust ourselves and flee from interactions with those who profess doctrines that are contrary to those of our Holy Mother Church.

As the fourth way to conserve the faith, let us point to the Christian courage to confess our sins. A Christian must never deny the faith, or even give the impression of doing so. He must always earnestly confess it as demanded by God's honor and the neighbor's salvation.

First, we can never deny, not even in appearance, that we believe in Jesus Christ and that we are the sons of the Catholic Church. The Church was established by him.

We cannot deny that we believe in all the truths that she puts forward for us to believe. We cannot do this for any motive, such as the acquisition of great wealth or of the entire world, or for the prevention of the loss of our belongings, health, or very life. Denying the faith is a grave offense against God, who is the truth itself, because it is the same as saying that he does not merit one's belief. Denying the faith is also the same as saying to Jesus Christ that we are ashamed to be his disciples, and for this he said, "For he that shall be ashamed of me and of my words, of him the Son of man shall be ashamed, when he shall come in his majesty, and that of his Father, and of the holy angels."[9]

We deny the faith not only with words, but also with actions, gestures, or a sign that expresses this denial. For thousands of martyrs, a single word, action, or gesture would have been enough to liberate them from suffering and death. But none of them did that, and so they gave glory to Jesus Christ and saved their souls. These Christian heroes also did not deny their faith in appearance, because they knew that this would cause great scandal, and would do grave injury to God even if they did not inwardly deny God. The beautiful example of the elderly Eleazar is celebrated everywhere. Those who loved him advised him that he only needed to appear to eat the prohibited meat in order to save his life. But he said, full of bravery, "For it doth not become our age, said he, to dissemble: whereby many young persons might think that Eleazar, at the age of fourscore and ten years, was gone over to the life of the heathens: And so they, through my dissimulation, and for a little time of a corruptible life, should be deceived, and hereby I should bring a stain and a curse upon my old age."[10] He said this, and

---

9   Luke 9:26.
10   2 Macc. 24–26.

died a glorious death, leaving this good example that so many have imitated since. Occasionally, tyrants force the martyrs to go in front of idols and put in their hands burning coal and incense so that, compelled by the pain, they would throw the coal and appear to offer incense to the idols. Taking the pain, they remained immobile so that they did not appear to offer incense through even the slightest hand movement.

What confusion and shame must these examples cause so many Christians who don't suffer for their faith neither a taunt or an insult! An impious satire, burlesque laughter, an overbearing look, or an insulting and bold phrase of enemies of religion are often enough to cause trembling among some Christians. These weak individuals should hear these words of Isaiah: "Fear ye not the reproach of men, and be not afraid of their blasphemies. For the worm shall eat them up as a garment: and the moth shall consume them as wool: but my salvation shall be for ever, and my justice from generation to generation."[11]

Neither can we deny the faith nor appear to do so in any case. But this is not enough. Instead, we must confess it, as we can conclude from St. Paul's words: "For, with the heart, we believe unto justice; but, with the mouth, confession is made unto salvation."[12] We can conclude the same from these words from Jesus Christ: "Every one therefore that shall confess me before men, I will also confess him before my Father who is in heaven."[13] In addition, the Church, founded by Jesus Christ, is a visible Church, and would no longer be visible if those who comprise it, in other words her children, do not confess her faith exteriorly. Just as someone who conceals his faith cannot be known as a disciple of Jesus Christ,

11   Isa. 51:7–8.
12   Rom. 10:10.
13   Matt. 10:32.

neither can the Church be known without the exterior confession of those who make up its membership.

There is, however, a difference in the obligations of not denying the faith from confessing the faith. We have said that never in any case can the faith be denied, not even in appearance. But in terms of confessing it exteriorly, it is not necessary for salvation to always do it, in every place and every circumstance, but only when the honor of God or the salvation of the neighbor demands it. When, then, our silence results in dishonor to God or in a bad example that can scandalize our neighbor, we are obliged to confess the faith, and we sin if we don't.

In our era, when we are obliged to live surrounded on all sides by the enemies of our holy religion, there are many occasions when we have the duty to confess our faith, under pain of sin. It is unfortunately not unheard of—and in fact frequent—that in our presence these enemies of our religion mock the holy mysteries, blaspheme our Lord Jesus Christ, insult our Holy Mother, ridicule the saints, deny some of the truths of the faith, such as the existence of hell (which so disturbs them), and other such things. In each and every one of these cases we are obliged to confess our faith, because God's honor requires and demands this, and our silence would be a guilty one.

But we do not intend to recommend the Christian courage for confessing the faith only when conscience obliges this, but also when there is no strict requirement to do so. We can often do this through our work. For example, we can receive the holy sacraments often even though they call us *pious*. We can attend the holy Mass, the Forty Hours Devotion, and other devotional acts, as much as our duties allow, even though they call us *slackers*. We can take part in an edifying way in processions and other religious rallies, even though they qualify us as *self-righteous*. We can revere those objects and people consecrated to God, even though they call us *clericalists*. We can help with the arrangement and decoration of the altars and churches, especially for important festivals, even though they call us *sacristans*. In contrast, we must reproach and reject all conduct and uttering that sounds like error and liberalism, and demonstrate our aversion to everything with the same sense, whether it concerns literature, school, college, association, a circle, and demonstration, an internment, a project, a company, or other such things.

The farther we can get away from error, the less danger we have of falling into it. If we succeed at feeling this aversion that I have just indicated for whatever smells or feels to be error, it will be a great security. It stays far away from us and is even a clear signal of the integrity of our faith. That's why we see liberal Catholics, for example, not feel any aversion to sins against the faith, which even seem for them to be insignificant. They are therefore scandalized when they hear that this sin is the gravest of all except for formal hate against God and total despair. This scandal reaches its height when, descending from this general proposition, we specify that being a rationalist, materialist, liberal, etc., is more sinful than being a drunk, thief, killer, or other such things. They cannot conceive of this, just like they fail to explain that God's servants fill with holy indignation when they see the spreading of heresy or the good faithful covering their ears after hearing a single word pronounced against the faith. They smile and think it's funny to see such manifestations of faith. That is why they do not feel horror at the sins against it. Having such a feeling, this horror, then, and feeling aversion to sins against the faith, and to everything that smells of error, is a good sign, and a great shield against heresy and error.

Let us have courage, then, my sons, Christian courage to confess the faith. It is an admirable way to conserve it and not lose it in the midst of so many dangers, and to ensure its expression, not only when we have the obligation to do so, but also on occasions such as what I mentioned before. In this way, you will position yourself farther from the danger and will be more secure from falling into it.

We believe, my sons, that if you come to properly practice things as I have just mentioned, telling things as they should be told, with the grace of God, which is never lacking, you will not have the great misfortune to lose faith and fall into the deep abyss of heresy. Take, then, in your practice, these ways. They will protect you from the evil impact of errors that have spread everywhere.

Don't be surprised that we insist so heavily on this matter of the conservation of the faith, or that we come back to this issue again and again. It is clear that today your situation is critical because the dangers that threaten your faith are much greater. You are neighbors of the unfortunate Republic of Ecuador, where masons, liberals, and every kind of enemy of our Lord Jesus Christ and his holy religion dominate and direct things. And because the horrible echoes of their blasphemy, heresies, and errors reach you, you must be prepared so that none of this stains or damages your faith in the least. In addition, your towns are inundated with books, leaflets, newspapers, and writings that these men send you. These are plagued with doctrinal errors and insults against our holy religion. Liberals are not lacking in each town who read these terrible writings. They speak in favor of this cause to you, and applaud and praise the writings. Currently, the Constitution of the Republic of Ecuador, produced at the revolutionary Convention, is passed from hand to hand, while liberals praise and recommend it. How can we allow them to deceive you? It is necessary that we say something about this Constitution, so that you will know what you are dealing with when you hear it being praised.

The Constitution that was given to Ecuador not only is not worthy of applause and praise, but also merits the anathema and reproach of every good Catholic because it contains dispositions that are highly injurious: 1) against God, whom it disdains in a most daring way, making him not equal but inferior to false gods because it allows the entry into Ecuador of the ministers of these, but not those of the true God; 2) against the Church of Jesus Christ, whose rights it violates and stamps on in a most scandalous manner; 3) against the religious orders, which are so loved by the Church for their important services, against which Ecuador's borders were closed despite being open to all the sectarian ministries; 4) against the faithful Ecuadorians, whose religion is despised, insulted, and persecuted; 5) against the nation, composed of an immense majority of Catholics, whose right not to have any other religion than Catholic, was not considered in any way, let alone protected.

Ecuador's revolution was the work of the masonic lodges. The Convention participants worked in such a way as to be able to say, "We followed your aims in persecuting Catholicism and in hating Jesus Christ. This, therefore, is the Constitution, the supreme law of the republic, against which God's laws, those of Jesus Christ, and those of his Church, had no effect on the text if they deviated from it." It was in vain that God, in his law, prohibited bad thoughts, words, and works, along with gatherings, associations, discourses, false worship, and writings contrary to this law, because Ecuador's supreme law gives freedom to all of this.

In vain did Jesus Christ order the Apostles and successors to preach the gospel to the whole world, and give his Church supremacy over the state, coercive and temporal power, immunity for its personnel, premises and goods, and the mission to teach everyone everything related to the salvation of men because Ecuador's supreme law orders the contrary. In vain does the same Church prohibit the dispossession of ecclesiastical goods, and nominate foreign church leaders, as it so pleases, for Ecuador's churches and convents, or give benefits as support, and condemn liberty of thought and word, the press, and teaching because all of these depart from the text of Ecuador's supreme law, and therefore have no effect.

What audacity, what boldness, and what delirium! What injury to God and to men! What heresy and what error! With what zeal would we show how perverse, absurd, and malicious is each provision of this supreme law. It is against the sacred laws. But it is not possible to do such in a pastoral letter. It requires a book, and not a small one, for enough information so that each Catholic can understand that it needs to be rejected.

You already know, my children, what you need to say to those who show you this Constitution and praise it. Tell them that it contains blasphemous, heretical, erroneous, injurious, evil, and scandalous provisions from the theological perspective; that it is a fertile origin of vice, apostasy, sin, and iniquity when considered from the moral perspective; and that it is the cause of sedition, disturbances, disorder, damage, and ruin for individuals, towns, and the nation from the political perspective.

I am sure that the supporters of error will ask us, as they already have on another occasion, why we get mixed up in foreign affairs. We respond that we do so because foreigners get mixed up in our affairs all the time with great nerve and the evilest intentions. These foreigners should leave us in peace, and not send even one of the many pages filled with anti-Catholic doctrines that they do send us. They should stop with their attempts to get believers to leave the faith. Perhaps then we will be quiet.

We say "perhaps," because anywhere we see persecution of the Church, we have the duty to defend her. If errors appear anywhere, we must combat them with our powers.

Faithful Christians, disciples of Jesus Christ, sons of the Catholic Church, you also have the duty to defend your godly Master and Mother Church. No: It is not only the bishops and priests who have to speak and work to fight the destructive currents of error, including freemasonry and its servant, liberalism, and to defend religion. The simple faithful must also do this through all legal means that are within their reach in the form and manner that they can.

If faithful Catholics worked to defend their religion as energetically as their enemies work to destroy it, we would certainly not have to lament so much persecution and misfortune as we do everywhere. It is so shameful to compare our enemies' persecution of religion with our own apathy and inertia in defending it! Let this conduct, which is cowardly and undignified for Catholics, be far from us. Let us fearlessly confess Jesus Christ in front of men. Let us courageously defend his holy Church. Let us be willing and able to suffer and lose everything instead of committing even the smallest of modern errors that are related to deathly liberalism. Let us not shy away from mockery, insults, and threats from the enemies of God, the Church, and society. Let us work in this way, and have no occasion to face the divine castigation that other people suffer or to let the following words of the Savior be fulfilled in us: "Therefore I say to you, that the kingdom of God shall be taken from you, and shall be given to a nation yielding the fruits thereof."[14]

We conclude, my children, in saying that, just as it is impossible to please God without having faith or to justify or save yourself, it is also impossible without faith

14   Matt. 21:43.

to receive the Holy Sacraments that the Church requires for us to receive in this holy time of Lent. Those, then, who accept an error condemned by the Church, must not approach the Holy Sacraments without first repenting and discarding the error. The sacraments, which are the springs of life and grace for those who receive them properly, transform into venom, death, and condemnation in those who receive them unworthily.

Oh divine faith! Come, Son of heaven, descend on us and spread throughout our minds your dazzling light, so that with it, in this holy time of Lent, we can penetrate into the sublime and loving mysteries of the Passion and Death of our sweet Jesus. Let us understand the treasures of salvation, grace, and blessing that his abundant redemption provides us. Let us strive to turn to these riches through the Holy Sacraments, which were instituted for this merciful end, and let us obtain the eternal salvation of our souls.

Let us strive to make the most of the fruits of redemption while there is still time. Let us receive with the proper disposition the Holy Sacraments and obtain the salvation of our soul. This is the only truly necessary thing necessary for man. This is what your bishop requests and begs. He blesses you in the name of the Father ✠ and of the Son ✠ and of the Holy Spirit ✠. Amen.

This pastoral letter is to be read in all the churches of our diocese on the two Feast Days during the Mass.

> Given and signed for Us without seal
> and countersigned by our secretary
> in Pasto on February 12, 1897.
> ✠ Fr. Ezequiel, *Bishop of Pasto;*
> *Anselmo Guerrero, Secretary.*

FIFTH
Pastoral Letter

THAT HIS EXCELLENCY THE BISHOP
OF PASTO SENDS TO THE VENERABLE
CLERGY AND FAITHFUL OF HIS DIOCESE,
ARRANGING FOR THE REPARATION FOR
THE PROFANING AND FOUL INSULT
OF THE HOLIEST SACRAMENTS IN
RIOBAMBA (ECUADOR).

To the venerable clergy and faithful of our diocese: good health and blessings in Our Lord Jesus Christ.

OUR CURRENT MONTH IS THE time of religious enthusiasm for the good faithful because June is when we celebrate the great Feast of Corpus Christi, the commemoration of the institution of the Most Holy Sacrament of the Eucharist. The month is also consecrated in a special way to the celebration of the Sacred Heart of Jesus. Fervent souls surrender themselves to the most tender worship of the Divine Heart of Jesus. They seek to console this Heart through their own wills with more sacrifices, mortifications, purity, burning love, repeated communion, and continuous acts of reparation for insults that, in its love, the Sacrament suffers.

After man had fallen into guilt and lost the heritage of the beautiful heaven that God had destined him for, the Eternal Word, the Son of God, had mercy on him, left his throne of glory, and came down to earth to become man to redeem him and to bring back the lost righteous. Our present purposes do not require every proof of the love that Jesus Christ provided to men in his thirty-three years among us. This evidence is found in the gospel, and it is enough to read it with good faith. We only wish to remind you a little what the gospel tells us about Christ's institution of the Holy Eucharist. This is to raise the matter of the cold ingratitude with which men respond to this gift of love of Jesus Christ. It is also to discuss the duty that we have to make reparations for the insults that were committed against this lovely Sacrament, which is a miracle of love.

Our Lord Jesus Christ, seeing that the hour was nearing when he would leave the world and return to his Heavenly Father, was seized by his love for men. He did not permit this love to be separated from them. Therefore, according to Tertullian's sublime phrase, *his heart calling from within his heart*, he took in his hands unleavened bread. He looked heavenward, let resonate his omnipotent voice that had declared, "Let there be" to create everything, and pronounced the solemn words, "Take and eat, this is my Body; take and drink, this is my Blood." He gave his whole self to his apostles in the Eucharist. In this way, Jesus Christ instituted an eternal memorial of his love for men, the august sacrament of the altar. There, it will stay with us until the end of time to keep us company so that we can visit, speak with, beg, and adore him. But the memorial will also offer him as a sacrifice in an unbloody way on our altars. This renews the bloody sacrifice of the Cross and mysteriously feeds our souls with his own flesh. It unites him with us in an intimate and ineffable way.

We call the sacrament of the Eucharist the "mystery of faith," but we can also call it the "mystery of love." Yes, the mystery of love is the sacred Eucharist. It is ardent, strong, and faithful. It is a full love, a love of friendship, sibling, father, and spouse. It is a generous love that gives everything because Jesus has given us everything in the Eucharist: his sacrosanct body, his precious blood, his blessed soul, his divinity with his infinite perfections. Can Jesus Christ give us more than he has given us in this sacrament? No, my great father St. Augustine responds without vacillation. Being omnipotent, he cannot give us more. Being the wisest, he does not know how to give us more. His treasures are the richest and inexhaustible. He therefore possesses nothing of greater value than that which he has given us.

If the faith does not testify to these truths, who could come to believe in them? If Jesus Christ had not carried out this miracle of love through his own election, who would have even imagined it, let alone asked for it. Oh, the immense goodness of our Divine Redeemer! Oh, the infinite love! Oh, the precious gift of the Eucharist! Whoever embraces it receives all of its goodness. There are no riches, treasures, beauties, happiness, or pleasures that can equal this gift. It is a miracle of divine love. Whatever heaven has that is great, majestic, lovely, beautiful, delightful, soft, sweet, or kind is ours to possess. We can rejoice about this because Jesus Christ gave us his whole being. There is nothing greater, richer, more excellent, or more worthy of adoration and love either in heaven or on earth.

What more can we say about the love of Jesus Christ in the Eucharist? We can speak of the effects and of the souls who experience it. But oh! we can say little, very little. Come, seraphim! You who, surrounding the throne of the glory of Jesus Christ, and say without ceasing: Holy, holy, holy! Come down to us, and in your heavenly words speak to us of the beautiful things, of the love, and of the affection of the Eucharist. Ah! You cannot tell us everything. You will never tell us because the infinite cannot be grasped by a creature, all the more since it is a seraphim burning with divine love. Oh, love! Oh love of Jesus! Let every tongue praise your immense goodness. Oh divine Redeemer! Let all honor, blessings, and glory be given to you!

Dear Christians! Does the loving Jesus not merit the eternal gratitude of men? After Jesus Christ gave us these proofs of his love, would we not expect men to give this gratitude in return, and feel their hearts burning with love for him? Can there be any other being who is so worthy of the love of men? Still men do not love Jesus Christ! Instead of giving thanks and love-filled praise, which is what we owe in return for his blessings, good works, and love, we express ingratitude, a scorching wind. Ingratitude is the root of all spiritual evil, as my spiritual father St. Augustine called it. It develops to the point of insulting Jesus Christ in the sacrament that is worthy of our adoration and the summation of his wisdom, power, and love. The soul fills with bitterness in thinking of this sad reality. Yes, forgetfulness, scorn, offense, rage, and cruelty are men's gratitude for the affection and delicate love of Jesus Christ, which he made into a sacrament for them.

Jesus is among us, but it seems that men know nothing of this beautiful and consoling truth. Who thinks of him? Who visits him? Who comes closer to the tabernacle, where he waits day and night? Oh, at certain times of the day, our churches are totally deserted, and Jesus, sweet Jesus, is alone, forgotten, and abandoned.

Jesus gives himself to us in the sacrament of life. He calls us. He searches for us, so that we receive him. He calls and seeks us, so that we can believe –oh, infinite goodness!— that we can believe that he misses and needs us. Who hears this call of love? How many receive him? Oh, such shame! The Church must require that we receive him once, at least once per year, and—oh the pain! Many

Christians do not receive him for one year at least, but some for two, twenty, thirty, or more years. Perhaps they have not received him since first communion when they were children. Now they are adults, old and close to standing before the One whom they would not receive when they were on earth!

Men's ingratitude for Jesus Christ in the sacrament goes beyond even what we have stated. It reaches irreverence and scorn. There are men who, in the presence of the consecrated Host, do not bend their knees. They still bend, but before whom? Some carry themselves in a way that would not be permitted if they were among half-cultured, half-educated men. Others are distracted, and look around in every direction, looking for idols to pay the demonstration of love that they owe Jesus Christ. Still others laugh, talk, and play in the presence of Jesus Christ in the sacrament, while the seraphim tremble and reverently prostrate themselves before his Divine Majesty.

Is this all? No. Jesus Christ is insulted even in the sacrament of his love, with sacrilegious communions, impious thefts, doubts about his real presence, and shameless denials of the Mystery, with ironic laughter, cruel mockery, and horrible blasphemy.

When we reflect on these indignities, we ask ourselves: "Will the offenses committed against Jesus Christ in the Holy Eucharist stop? Oh, the pain! Appalling events signal that this will not stop; that men even feel hate, rage, fury, and cruelty for Jesus Christ. Yes, men go so far as to have cruelty for the sweet and meek Jesus, who so loved and loves them.

Why should we be quiet when, nearby and hardly a month ago, men showed us this hate, anger, rage, and cruelty for Jesus Christ in the sacrament? Why should we be quiet when the enemies of Jesus Christ are not content with killing one of his servants, injuring another, and imprisoning a virtuous and courageous bishop? Jesus in the sacrament is the target of the most despicable mockery, boldest insults, and most criminal offenses. Why should we be quiet when they are not content with profaning a temple and smashing up the images of the saints and Our Lady, breaking up the tabernacle, and with furious rage and spontaneous cruelty squeezing between their hands the Divine Sacrament. They threw the sacred forms on the ground and trampled them. They ate them with infernal temerity, and then drank brandy from the sacred vessels. Great God! Where is your power, this power that fills the deep with fright and checks the storms? Where is this voice that flattens the seemingly-eternal hills and knocks down the centuries-old cedars? Ah! Your patience is more, much more admirable than man's wickedness is horrible, but you are—oh, my God!—you are patient because you are eternal. You do nothing more than hope a little.

You well know, my children, that these horrendous sacrileges took place last month in the village of Riobamba in the neighboring republic of Ecuador. You have read about them in the newspapers or at least you've heard of these.

In view of this horrible scene of profanation, blood, and impiety, let us see if we were correct in saying at another time that liberalism is REBELLION AGAINST GOD, and as a consequence, very bad. It is the great calamity of the present age. It is the great evil that threatens to destroy everything, including the annihilation of the entire religious, political, and social orders. What the liberals have done recently in Ecuador, they did before in Colombia. It is what liberals everywhere have done and still do today because the damned tree of liberalism can give no other fruits.

What's more, the liberals among us even dare to say that our holy father Leo XIII praises and blesses liberalism! Be quiet, fools, and stop insulting in this way the old and wise pontiff who called liberals IMITATORS OF THE DEVIL. Addressing Catholics who call themselves liberals, he spoke these words that we recall once again in order to set right the authors of this insult: "We cannot understand how there are people who call themselves Catholics and at the same time not only have sympathies for liberalism, but also have such a level of blindness and foolishness that they glory in calling themselves liberals" (Address to the Consistory of Cardinals, June 30, 1889).[1] If only sympathy for liberalism, or the mere name "liberal," warrants such censure from the Holy Father, how much more offended will someone be if the pope has blessed liberalism?

In the *Syllabus*, which liberals find so disturbing, the Church has solemnly condemned modern liberalism. We cannot be under any illusions or hope that liberals will start to say something else. To remove all hope for liberals of reconciliation with the Church, let us use a noble phrase from sacred scripture to say that once the Church has condemned liberalism, she has condemned it FOR ALL OF ETERNITY, AND EVEN BEYOND: IN AETERNUM ET ULTRA.

I now turn to you who, in this horrible confusion and apostasy, remain faithful to Jesus Christ and his Church. What do you say about the wrongs done to Jesus Christ in Riobamba? What do you say when you see Jesus in the most holy sacrament thrown on the ground, stomped on, eaten as sacrilege, offended, vilified, mocked? What do you say when you know and meditate on the fact that it was done with anger, fury, rage, and cruelty that is unworthy of men? The God vilified in Riobamba is our God. What can we do about such affronts and

---

1   These words are actually found in the Encyclical *Libertas*. [German translator.]

punishable attacks on the tender, soft, and loving Jesus in the sacrament? Do these impious attacks and despicable treatments not move our hearts and fill us with hurt in a most intimate way? Will we be indifferent, cold, and frosty knowing of these horrendous crimes of HATE against God, these crimes which targeted Jesus Christ in the sacrament of his love, these crimes that seem fitting only for Satan? O most sweet Jesus! Why has it not been given to us to shed torrents of tears and for such horrendous crimes to be washed and expiated with our own blood and lives? With how many reasons—oh our Savior!—with how many reasons did you make your faithful spouse, the blessed Margarita Maria, hear your heartfelt complaint: "Here is the Heart that has loved men so much, who, to show his love, did not fail to forgive everyone until the point of becoming small and being consumed. Instead of appreciation, I receive nothing more than ingratitude, contempt, irreverence, and sacrilege in the sacrament of my love!"

After this complaint, he asked his servant to offer solace to his Heart as an act of reparation, and above all for a public apology on the first Friday after the Octave of Corpus Christi. He promised those who offer communion on this day, in reparation for the offenses that he received during the Octave, that at this exposition at the altars he will pour over them his love in abundance.

The God OF ALL CONSOLATION asks for consolation for his Heart! Will we be so indifferent and hard-hearted that we will not give this? Will we do nothing to repair the injuries that the sacrament continually receives in his love? Above all, will we do nothing to make reparations for the anger, fury, cruelty, and hate with which the sacrilegious of Riobamba have treated him? Oh! No, let us not imitate these Catholics who hear repeatedly of these horrendous scenes, as they read and hear of certain other things, and like them not be affected by the abuses of ministers of the altar, of religion, and of God himself.

We must also not listen to those who say that we must come to accept the circumstances. This implies that we must resign ourselves to quietly witness the iniquitous war against Jesus Christ and everyone who is connected to him. Cowards! These Catholics don't want to suffer anything for he who suffered so much for them. They are scared off by ridicule, insults, slurs, and fury from the enemies of God. What would happen to Catholicism if the pope, bishops, priests, and good faithful accommodated themselves to the circumstances and remained silent when errors and persecutions arose against the Church? The sheer thought of the consequences that would follow from this cowardly and shameful conduct brings a sense of horror. What is needed, then, in these cases is to make use of all legal means to oppose evil. It is necessary, at least, to protest, even if no other thing can be done.

We protest, then, against the barbarian indignities that the liberals of Riobamba did to Our Lord Jesus Christ, and we do everything possible to make reparations to him and to console him. The occasion could not be more propitious because the day of the Sacred Heart is near, and it is a great day of reparation chosen by the same Jesus Christ. On this great day, the august solemnity of the Feast of Corpus Christi, with its octave, in which we have the special veneration of the Most Holy Sacrament, which was so vilely profaned in Riobamba. Everyone is thus invited so that we can do many fervent acts of reparation. But we desire to do something special as a solemn protest against the impious and barbaric acts of Riobamba. With this in mind, we have determined to celebrate the following functions:

1. On the 23, 24, and 25, the acts of reparation will be celebrated in the Cathedral, with the exposition of the Most Holy Sacrament, from six in the morning until night; solemn Mass will be at nine the next day, and at five the rosary, a sermon, and the Trisagion with singing to the Sacred Heart of Jesus, followed by investiture. In the afternoon of the last day, instead of the distribution, a customary procession with our Most Holy Sacrament will take place.

2. We give the necessary permission so that in churches in this city, and after the Triduum in the cathedral, worship with the exposition of the Most Holy Sacrament can be celebrated. With greater passion for this, greater and greater reparations can be made to the Sacred Heart of Jesus.

3. In every place throughout the whole diocese, the senior priests who have the means to do so will celebrate a solemn Triduum with exposition of the Most Holy, and in those parishes that do not have the means, one day or whatever can be given with the goal of reparations to Our Lord Jesus Christ.

So that Jesus Christ is well-accompanied in these days in which he is exposed to the veneration of the faithful, we ask for directors of associations to allocate a half hour to each choir, or part of each, so they can alternate in going to the adoration of Our Most Holy. The priests can do the same in schools, colleges, and even families who contribute to giving tribute to the King of glory. Christian souls! Accompany Jesus Christ on these days of reparation! Let nothing be lacking in giving him glory! Do not expect that someone will look for or invite you, because it is not possible to come to imagine that it is

Jesus Christ who needs you, and not you him, or that he is worth a little and you a lot!

Pray willingly to offer what you can to make reparations to our Jesus in the Sacrament! Let there be religious zeal in giving honor to the consecrated Host! May there be a large turnout to the processions and religious acts! May there be an abundance of lights, flowers, decorations, flags, and arches of triumph for the King of the centuries! Above all, my children, may there be an exuberance of faith, profound veneration, reparative communion, and love, much love for our good Jesus in the Sacrament! Honor and glory to Jesus in the Sacrament! Blessed and praised be the Most Holy Sacrament of the altar for eternity! May the Most Holy Sacrament of the altar be blessed and praised countless times!

We grant forty days of indulgence of each act of adoration and reparation before the presence of Jesus in the Sacrament throughout the entire Octave of Corpus Christi, in the Feast of the Sacred Heart of Jesus, and in the days that the acts of reparation are held for the purpose already mentioned.

This pastoral letter will be read in all of the churches of the diocese on the first two days of the feast after it is received.

Given in Pasto, June 12, 1897.
✠ Fr. Ezequiel, *Bishop of Pasto;*
Anselmo Guerrero, Secretary.

SIXTH
Pastoral Letter

OF THE MOST REVEREND BISHOP OF
PASTO FOR LENT, 1898. HE SHOWS
THEREIN THAT NATIONS AND
INDIVIDUALS, INFECTED WITH
THE PLAGUE OF LIBERALISM, ARE
CASTIGATED BY GOD FOR THE
MOST COMPLETE ABANDONMENT
OF THE RELIGIOUS, MORAL,
POLITICAL, AND SOCIAL ORDER.

To the venerable clergy and children of our diocese:
greetings and blessings in our Lord Jesus Christ.

WITH THIS PASTORAL LETTER, we announce to you, our beloved children, the coming of Lent. As you know, this is a time which our holy mother Church dedicates in a special way to penance, and during which she calls out to her children more strongly than in the rest of the year and teaches them the ways of eternal salvation more frequently.

Yes, from the first day of Ash Wednesday in holy Lent, the Church does not cease to call out with a terrifying voice: Remember, you are ashes and to ashes you will return! Remember, you will die! Remember that judgment, hell, glory, and eternity exist! Convert to God! Do penance! Save your soul!

The Church calls out in this way in the time of Lent. Its ministers—bishops, priests, and missionaries—repeat these same cries everywhere. Let these cries be heard in the great cities just as in the small villages. The same goes for those who give orders as for those who obey, and equally for the learned as for the ignorant, the rich and poor, and the young and old because everyone will die, will give a strict account of all his deeds to God, and will be sentenced either to enjoy God in heaven for eternity in the company of the holy Virgin and the saints, or to suffer in hell for all of eternity in the company of demons and the condemned.

To today's society and those who say and write, as it was said and written among us, that *the theater is like the air that the soul must breathe*; to those who get excited by frequent bouts of drinking and the satisfaction of fleshly appetites; to those who desire and seek a life of pleasure and material happiness, this reminder of death, judgment, hell, and eternity from our holy mother the Church and its ministers must seem in very poor taste. Today it is not pleasing to hear talk of these things. The delicate and polite sentiments of this epoch do not accept this language.

Indeed, many people want the effeminacy that is spreading everywhere to be introduced into the Church itself, and that papal encyclicals, bishops' letters, and priests' sermons all be literature, eloquence, and flowery but insubstantial talk, and that nothing be said of eternal punishments or be tough and powerful. When they therefore hear things called by their proper name, that evil is evil and good, good; when they hear a totally clear protest against errors, vices, and worldly distractions that pull the soul down into damnation; when they hear the threat of God's judgment and of the eternal punishment that is reserved for those who offend and insult him; and when they hear, I say, this language of truth, they cannot hold back. They call those who speak like this deceptive, regressive, ignorant, unrefined, uneducated, and deserving to live among savages instead of among the fully enlightened and civilized who have such excellent social skills as do those of this era of progress. In the event that one starts speaking to them of God (for even this needs to be sparing), it has to be *this God of theirs*, who is good, merciful, sweet, full of charity. But this is *not our God*, who on the one hand is good and merciful, but on the other is just, strong, jealous of his honor, and a terrible avenger of outrages that occur. *Loquimini nobis placentia.* Speak to us of pleasant things, and prophesy of happy things, even if they are false. Here is the modern spirit. Here are what men who are filled with this spirit desire and request.

No, the men of modern progress do not want to hear talk of threats and punishments. Yet we must speak to them of this, because the peoples and individuals infected by the terrible plague of liberalism can only expect punishment. Yes, God does threaten a great punishment for those peoples and individuals who mock and abandon him. This punishment is the abandonment of what they have left behind in the religious, moral, political, and social orders. This is what we wish to show on the present occasion. May heaven grant this to be beneficial for souls.

I

"Men are born and remain free." So declares the first article of the famous "Declaration of the rights of man." Liberals repeat this. It is the cry of rebellion of liberalism itself. It is Lucifer's *I will not serve*.

Our holy mother Church, and Catholics along with her, declares that "men are born and remain dependent" because they are created. Dependency is an aspect of the very essence of man because his essence is to be a creature, and the creature necessarily depends on his Creator. God, then, as man's Creator, is Master and Lord of what man possesses. Everything that man can think, desire, and do must be for God because nothing belongs to man, and everything is from God. For this the Psalmist says, "All my bones shall say: Lord, who is like to thee?" (Ps. 34:10). For the same reason, God begins his Ten Commandments with these words: "I am the Lord thy God" (Exod. 20:2). Here we have the reason why God imposed his law on man. He is our Lord, and can command us as his servants. We must obey the law as such. We must place in his service everything that we have because everything is his. It would be theft to hold back the smallest thing.

It is not only that. We must also offer the service that we owe God, our Lord and Master, not as it pleases us, but as defined by *the only true and obligatory* religion as promulgated by our Lord Jesus Christ for all of humanity. This is because Jesus Christ, as God and as sent by God, can prescribe and did indeed prescribe, the way for men to serve God and worship him in a way that pleases him.

Jesus Christ, the One who was sent, had to leave the earth and return to his Heavenly Father who had sent him. He therefore established a Church. He gave it the divine mission of teaching men to do all of that He ordained to offer to God the worship that is due. The Church fulfills this mission through its visible head and its ministers who teach and preach the doctrines of Jesus Christ, administer the holy sacraments that he instituted, gather together the faithful for the offering of the divine sacrifice and liturgical prayers, give worship to the Highest, and elevate hearts to him with rites that are as majestic as they are simple. The Council of Trent declares, "It is not in man's nature to easily elevate himself to contemplate divine things without the help of exterior things. The Church was therefore moved to establish sacred rites. Through them she makes holy things desirable, and the sight of these pious and religious signs causes the spirits of the faithful to contemplate the most sublime mysteries." (Session 22, Chapter 5).

Everything in the religion that was established by Jesus Christ our Lord, who is Son of the Living God, sent by the Father and Savior of the world, is beautiful, great, and elevated. In this religion, God is properly adored, honored, and glorified. By paying his tributes to *the true God who is worthy of infinite honor,* man is far from humbling himself. He makes himself king because "to serve God is to rule," and even to make oneself a kind of God. According to the Psalmist, "You are gods." What could be a more glorious gift for man? All the grandeur of the wealthiest is truly baseness and nothing can be compared to such elevated servitude. Furthermore, for this honorable servitude, man merits and attains the vision, possession, and enjoyment of God for all of eternity.

Liberalism converts all of this beauty, attractiveness, and harmony of the religious order into ugliness, horror, and confusion when it proclaims its disastrous liberties and makes men independent of God. "Everyone says they are free to decide in religious matters according to their understanding, and can licitly embrace their preferred religion, or follow no religion if none satisfies them."[1] They also say, "There is therefore no reason to become attached to certain supernatural practices, nor work towards extravagant goals, nor waste time with the sacraments, saints' days, ridiculous processions and practices, that are repelled by reason." Does this not merit punishment?

II

Yes, God punishes these men who abandon him and call themselves free by abandoning them and disgracing them in the religious order. They do not want to adore and worship the *true God who is infinite in every class*

---

1 Pope Leo XIII, *Immortale Dei.*

85

of perfection. They adore *finite and imperfect things*, and are therefore castigated and disgraced.

Liberalism rebels against God, gives to man the independence that belongs only to God, and proclaims man to be God. "There is no longer any other worship, nor any other religion, than the religion of reason and the worship of liberty" (Amadeo Jacques). "There is in each of us an ideal that is superior to Golgotha" (Feuerbach). "The adoration of man must replace that of God" (Idem). Punishment!...Disgrace for these men!...They have exchanged God for man, the Creator for the creature, the infinite for the finite!

Another liberal god is "the people." This is the "sovereign," who desires, lives, and reigns. We must follow "the will of the people." The people decide and command, and what it decides is law, and what it commands must be done. Nothing can be done if it is not desired and commanded by the people. The people instead of God! Punishment!...Disgrace!

"Humanity." Here is another liberal god. "Oh Queen Humanity! It is your time!" (Littré). "Humanity is definitively put in the place of God" (The New Thinking). In some places it has gotten to the point that alms "for Humanity" are collected, with the claim "that Humanity will reward you." Until now alms were requested "for the love of God," and it was said "that God rewards charity." Poor and miserable humanity, who at the level of individual people have to resort to begging for alms, takes the place of God, who is infinitely rich, at the altar!...Punishment!...Tremendous disgrace!

The liberals at the lodges worship the sun, fire, and the natural realm. They have returned to paganism! Disgrace!...Yes, disgrace and punishment!

But punishment and disgrace should be even greater. Yes, an even greater disgrace because to adore the sun or fire, wooden or marble statues, serpents or dogs, plants or trees, is to adore Lucifer.... This is a greater disgrace than that of the Egyptians who adored onions!... Lucifer is honored and exalted in the interiors of the lodges, and sometimes in the streets and plazas, by men who call themselves free. A few years ago his image was triumphantly paraded in the streets of Rome itself, and a few months ago this occurred in Buenos Aires. Terrible punishment! Dreadful disgrace! God abandons in the religious order those who declare themselves free and independent of his domination.

III

Those who rebel against God and do not subject themselves to his commandments that he gave to all men so that they live a just and perfect life are also punished and disgraced in the moral order so that they can merit the supernatural and happy end for which they were created.

Catholic morality is the purest and holiest of all moral teachings that the world has ever seen because it alone has as its author the essence of sanctity. There is no virtue that this morality does not recommend, nor any vice that it does not reprove, nor passion that it does not teach to dominate, nor state whose duties it does not explain, nor social class that it abandons. It eradicates evil from the root, going so far as to prohibit bad thoughts. It has the means to elevate man to a perfection of life that loves and captivates. It has indeed created and developed countless men of sanctity who became like angels who walk over the land and fill the world with a just, well-deserved, and immortal fame.

Liberalism tends by its nature to destroy whatever Catholic morality built, and to stain and disfigure what it made beautiful. Instead of this elevated and holy morality, it proclaims "independent morality." "Morality must be independent of all divine and ecclesiastical authority."[2] As a logical consequence, this independent morality is not understood by everyone in the same way. It stands more or less in opposition to Catholic morality according to the greater or lesser degree of liberalism professed by its advocates. The most extreme understand independent or free morality as "the emancipation of the passions," which in reality is "the negation of all morality."

God punishes these free men for their abandonment of the moral order. They end up humbled and enslaved by the rebellion of their passions against the spirit. St. Paul declares, "Who changed the truth of God into a lie; and worshiped and served the creature rather than the Creator, who is blessed for ever. Amen. For this cause God delivered them up to shameful affections...to a reprobate sense."[3]

IV

These words of the apostle clearly express how God will abandon those who abandon him. This is the great punishment that God commands for the sinner. The major evidence of his just anger is that he permits that a sin be punished by another sin. God is the source of all justice and cannot participate in sin. Sin always emerges from human malice. But God can permit most justly that a sin be punished by another, as he abandons those who abandon him as punishment for ingratitude, pride, and rebelliousness.

The extreme degradation that many have reached nowadays can only be explained as the effect of this abandonment. They are no longer content with their own corruption, but strive with determination to corrupt others. We hear how a leader of the *Carbonari*[4] expresses himself: "In

---

2   *Syllabus*, Proposition 57.
3   Rom. 1:25, 26, 28.
4   Italian secret brotherhood of the nineteenth century.

our discussions, we decided that we no longer want to be Christians. We popularize vice among the masses, that they may use their five senses; that they may drink, that they may get their fill.... We never get tired of corrupting others.... Let men form hearts of vice, and no longer be Catholics.... We dedicate ourselves to corruption on a great scale, the corruption of the people through the clergy, and the clergy through us. This corruption that we bring is meant to bury the Church. Recently, I heard our friend laughing at our projects and saying, *To destroy Catholicism, you need to start by eliminating women.* This phrase is true in a certain manner. But because we cannot eliminate women, we will corrupt them along with the Church.... The best dagger for injuring the heart of the Church is corruption. Let's get on with this work until we finish" (Letter from Vindex to Nuvio, cited by Crétineau-Joly).

Masonry, the excommunicated sect that worships Lucifer, the master of corruptors, can offer nothing more than corruption and more corruption. To do this, free men support the impious press; distribute everywhere dirty brochures, vile magazines, and books that are filled with horrendous blasphemy; support theaters and gatherings that endanger modesty; promote pleasures of every sort; energize the vilest passions; multiply centers of corruption; and organize a treasonable and iniquitous persecution against the work of Jesus Christ. While with his higher morality the Divine Savior raises men to an elevated, supernatural, and divine world, Lucifer's imitators sink down into a revolting mire of vice, evil, and crime. But what shame for these men! What humbling does the office of the corruptor bring! Could there be a greater punishment and deeper humbling than to be the supporter of the devil in the destruction of souls? Still, they put on a display of their vile and degrading office! This display of shamelessness is a greater, a much greater, punishment. The wretches!

"For he must reign, until he hath put all his enemies under his feet."[5] Thus declared the apostle, inspired by the Holy Spirit, and so it will happen. As much as his enemies dislike it, Jesus Christ will reign until the last day, when he will completely triumph over his enemies and set them under his feet. Then will this current way of reigning change into something spiritual and more elevated, an object of eternal happiness for the elect, with the Father and Holy Spirit. But he also reigns in the meantime: "He, Christ, must reign." King of kings and Lord of lords, he has the right to reign over every tribe, language, and nation.[6] Jesus Christ has the right to reign in public institutions and private customs, in temples and houses, in streets and squares, in schools and universities, in tribunals of justice and legislative bodies, in agreements of municipalities and resolutions of higher lawmakers.

But Jesus Christ as *the One Sent*, also has *that which he has sent*, which is the Church. He has given the Church the mission of guiding all men to their supernatural end. He has invested it with supreme authority over individuals, families, and states in everything that relates to the accomplishment of his mission. "Everything that is sacred in the life of humans, whatever it is called, everything that concerns the salvation of souls of worship of God, whether from its own nature, or in relation to something, everything is subjected to the judgment and power of the Church."[7] "The Church is a true and perfect society that is completely free. It enjoys its own and unchanging right that its Divine Founder conferred on it. No earthly power can limit its rights nor mark the limits of where

5   1 Cor. 15:25.
6   Rev. 5:9.
7   *Immortale Dei.*

these rights can be exercised." This is Catholic doctrine. The contrary is condemned.[8]

Moreover, "nowadays there is a tendency of ideas and the will to completely remove the Church from society."[9] Liberalism not only denies the supremacy of Jesus Christ and his Church over the state, but also claims the subjection of the Church to the state: "Liberals claim that ecclesiastical power cannot exercise authority except with the concession and approval of the state."[10] They also desire that legislation be free and independent of Jesus Christ and his Church. "Civil laws can and must be independent of divine and ecclesiastical authority."[11] Liberals go on to claim that in the past, everything depended on Biblical and ecclesiastical law; today it is necessary to establish laws on foundations that dispense with all belief. Everything must be free, and modern laws must be determined with freedom, founded on liberty, and oriented to the liberty of citizens in their social relations and family and individual acts as the goal.

This is how liberalism speaks, and therefore how the nations are governed "entirely independently of God and his Church." God in turn abandons to the political and social orders those who abandon him in this way. This abandonment from God is a punishment that humbles them and fills them with confusion and shame.

VI

Centuries have passed since the prophet Jeremia declared: "O Lord the hope of Israel: all that forsake thee shall be confounded: they that depart from thee, shall be written in the earth: because they have forsaken the Lord, the vein of living waters."

8   *Syllabus*, Proposition 19.
9   *Immortale Dei*.
10 *Syllabus*, Proposition 20.
11 *Syllabus*, Proposition 57.

Liberal minions, who abandon God and do nothing in his service when they are governing the peoples, see themselves, as the prophet says, disgraced and punished in this government. Liberal government is already disgraceful, because its *Yes* and *No* amount to the same thing. This is a contradiction, an absurdity. What is the law within liberalism? It is a contradiction with its liberties. What is an offense in liberalism? With its liberties, there are none. There cannot be any. What is justice in liberalism? Brute force. What is punishment in liberalism? Cruelty and nothing more because there are no crimes.

"Conscience" is just as free and sacred with those who make the law as with those who break it. "Opinion" is as free and sacred in those who apply punishment as in those who are believed to have committed a crime. Those who give the law and those who break it allege in their favor the same law: "his free conscience," "free opinion," and "free thought." All of this is as sacred for the one side as for the other. The one side takes liberty to mean that it is necessary to punish the thief, the murderer, the rebel, while the other uses the same liberty to claim that all of these crimes can be done legally, even going so far as to argue, like the anarchist, that starting fires, destroying, and killing people are virtues.

Punishment and prohibition of one of these ideas would be the absolute denial of the principle of liberty of conscience, opinion, and thought. Let us say: A liberal government is already a disgrace because it is a contradiction, a folly, and even more, an evil thing. It is evil not only for being anti-Catholic, but also for being anti-human and, as a consequence, antisocial. Therefore, this contradictory, disastrous, evil, anti-Catholic, anti-human, and antisocial government cannot give any other results than those that it brings, which are revolution, anarchy, despotism, and slavery. With all these plagues and more, we see the people who abandon God in order to follow modern liberties punished and disgraced.

The history of liberalism is only the history of revolutions. Even in times of apparent peace, we see an abnormal state, one we can call continual alarm, because it obliges governments to sustain armies that destroy the nations.

God humbles and crushes the pride of modern politicians, as Leo XIII notes: "Force alone will remain to preserve public tranquility and order. But force is very feeble when the bulwark of religion has been removed. Being more apt to beget slavery than obedience, it bears within itself the germs of ever-increasing troubles. The present century has encountered memorable disasters, and it is uncertain whether equally terrible disasters are on the horizon or not."[12]

The disturbances do not cease because their cause does not cease. Far from ending these disturbances, they become deeper and more disastrous each time. Anarchism is liberalism's legitimate consequence. Or, better put, anarchism is the purest, most refined liberalism, the essence of liberalism, and — odd thing! — these pure and clear liberals make liberal governments tremble. They have reason to tremble because punishment and disgrace sweep over the nations that abandon God. The consequences of liberalism are unavoidable and include assassinations, robberies, fires, ruins, confusion, dismay, dread, blood, and death. Anarchism arrives, but furiously, and this hellish miscarriage of liberalism will punish those who gave it life. Liberalism brings its punishment in its own horrendous sin. It is a wild beast that devours itself.

Anarchy always produces despotism. Those who do not want to carry the sweet yoke and light load of the Lord suffer the weight of the works of a certain slavery. This was the situation in the past, and will occur in

---

12   Pope Leo XIII, *Sapientiae Christianae.*

the future. When societies find themselves in agony, throw themselves into the arms of the first bold leader who presents himself as a liberator. Then, to sustain his power, this leader uses fetters and chains on those who previously called themselves free, and turns them into slaves. This is God's punishment, even in this world, of the proud who abandon God. This is the shame and disgrace that they fall into.

VII

We have shown you, beloved children, how, in the religious, moral, political, and social orders, God abandons and punishes individuals and peoples who have abandoned him so that they can live according to modern liberties. They do not take into account his teachings and commandments.

Many men refuse to worship and serve the thrice-holy God who created them and who preserves and destines them to a blessed eternity if they faithfully serve him. They have fallen into a deep disgrace of paying homage to any creature, and even to Lucifer himself, who is the father of evil who deceives and brings people to eternal damnation. At the same time that they sing of progress, they return to pagan idolatry and find themselves confused and humbled in their pride and rebellion.

They do not want to obey God's commands, nor follow Jesus Christ's sublime and holy morality. This morality makes men virtuous, perfect, and even happy to the extent that they can be in this world, and gives eternal happiness as the reward for faithfulness in this world. Their moral independence not only makes them corrupt, but also corruptors of others. This is the height of vileness, degradation, and monstrosity.

Modern politicians abandon God and want to govern societies not only independently of his doctrines and the laws of his holy Church, but also declare a more or less open war on all of the supernatural. They proclaim the empire of reason and secularize everything that they can. God has punished, abandoned, and disgraced them. He openly highlighted their impotence when they try to properly govern people with laws that change with the continuous fluctuation in men's opinions. They fluctuate because they are not based on the eternal. They contradict the liberties that they proclaim, and produce only anarchy and the ruin of the nations. Yes, it is a great shame and humiliation for proud modern politicians to see that at the same time that they proclaim every type of liberty, they see themselves obligated to establish violent policies supported by brute force and ever-larger armies. The greater the scorn they have for God's laws, the greater anarchy, despotism, slavery, and misfortune of every type emerge, along with a larger permanent army, as necessary consequences.

VIII

Please Lord, in your infinite mercy, free us of such horrible punishments. But we fear a great deal because God is greatly offended, and there is much contempt for his commandments and teachings. Liberalism has brought us a frightening confusion of ideas and a saddening and distressing moral situation of customs. Even many of those who pride themselves on being in the camp that is not Jesus Christ's enemy fit into the practices of this time and practice a superficial religion only so that they are not called nonbelievers. They make their way in the world without anyone gossiping about them. Taking from religion what they want, and discarding what they do not, they create a religion of their preferences that is easy and comfortable, that does not demand any sacrifices, that lets them fraternize easily with every kind of idea and opinion, read prohibited books, participate in theaters and dances, and every type of worldly distraction and fleshly satisfaction. These people are often "little content with their condition as subjects of the Church, believe that they can take some part in its governing, or think at least that it is licit to examine and judge the acts of authority in their own way."[13] In their pride they think that they alone are wise, and tell the popes and bishops how to act. They warn them and even at times provoke demonstrations of "public opinion" in order to impede certain things from happening or at least to discredit certain actions and decisions or to get certain agreements or toleration.

What does this conduct, so common in the men of today yet so little to do with the Catholic name that they give themselves, say and teach us? Oh! This conduct says and teaches us that liberalism has penetrated into these men without their awareness, that this destructive plague has spread, and that it is doing more damage than many think. The enemy is winning. He is winning because many Catholics have been obliging to him. They have not looked at hell's nefarious work. They walk arm in arm with Lucifer's imitators, and even when they say that they reject his ideas, they help and favor him in their actions. They have opened the door with their deference, public practices, and sins.

If we add to all of this the dissemination of pernicious ideas through so many corrupting books, dirty brochures and magazines, and frenzied voices of impiety and anarchism, we should not be surprised that our peoples go with haste towards the abyss of error and misfortune. Nor should we be surprised at the volcanic eruption that we felt so powerfully beneath our feet and that enveloped us in its destructive lava.[14]

13   Letter of Pope Leo XIII to Cardinal Guibert, June 17, 1885.
14   This may be metaphorical language, though an active volcano is nine kilometers south of Pasto. [German translator's note.]

It's been a while since one felt the just hand of God on the nation. We have pointed out on various occasions, just like the preachers of the truth have done, that stopping or evading the blow of divine anger requires works of penance. But some have contested these cries of anguish with foolish insults, others with foolish exuberance. Instead of shedding many tears over the nation's misfortune, they have eagerly sought foolish pleasure. They have made jokes out of commandments and preaching. They have publicly violated moral behavior, and have drunk sins like water. What should we expect if we don't humbly and contritely turn to God? We can only expect his abandonment of us because this is the punishment that nations who scorn him are threatened with. "Therefore I say to you, that the kingdom of God shall be taken from you, and shall be given to a nation yielding the fruits thereof" (Matt. 21:43).

Let us therefore return to God with sincere repentance for the offenses that we have committed. The holy time that approaches us invites us to a true conversion. We must respond to this invitation as is necessary to the salvation of our souls in order to appease God's anger and move away from these types of dangers that menace our faith. Let us humbly confess our sins. Let God hear the sighs of our hearts. Let us implore his goodness with unanimous and fervent prayer. This is our duty as Catholics. Let us fulfill it. Even when punishment comes, we will have the inner satisfaction of having tried to appease the Lord. We will be able to avoid the cries and mortification of our consciences and the responsibility for the calamities that come upon our nation, towns, and families and friends. May the Lord, beloved children, give you abundant and effective grace so that you may work in this manner, and serve him and give him glory, and save your souls. This is what your bishop desires, who blesses you in the name of the Father ✠ and of the Son ✠ and of the Holy Spirit ✠. Amen.

This pastoral will be read in all of the churches of our diocese on feast days after the first gospel of the Mass.

Given and undersigned for us, sealed with our seal, and countersigned by our secretary, in Pasto, on the day of St. Paul's Conversion, January 25, 1898.
✠ Fr. Ezequiel, *Bishop of Pasto*. Sent by the Reverend Anselmo Guerrero, Secretary.

EIGHTH
Pastoral Letter

IN WHICH THE BISHOP PRAISES THE
GLORIES OF THE VIRGIN OF LAS LAJAS
AND ORDERS THAT A COLLECTION BE
TAKEN UP IN ALL THE CHURCHES OF
THE DIOCESE IN ORDER TO BUILD A
NEW CHURCH DEDICATED TO HER.

*To the venerable clergy and faithful of our Diocese, greet-
ings and blessings in our Lord Jesus Christ.*

Thou art the glory of Jerusalem, thou art the joy of
Israel, thou art the honor of our people.
Jth. 15:10

WHEN OUR LORD JESUS CHRIST
was hanging on the Cross on the top of
Mount Calvary and was about to hand over
his spirit to the Father, not having anything else to give
us because he had already given us everything he had, he
opened his divine mouth and gave us his own mother
as our mother. From this supreme moment onwards,
those redeemed by the precious blood shed by the Divine
Savior felt the urgent and, at the same time, the sweet
and consoling necessity to approach the tender embrace
of this mother and turn to her love in all their pains
and tribulations.

Since then Christianity has seen itself drawn to Mary
and understands that her Holy Son made her treasurer
of heaven and wants all grace that comes from heaven

to earth to pass through her hands. From this comes the great enthusiasm for serving, praising, and blessing her, and the determined commitment to build churches, sanctuaries, chapels, and altars to her. These were and are places of charm and sweet attraction. Those who in this vale of tears make pilgrimages to these places encounter rest from their fatigue. They feel the holiness and consolation that give them the courage and force to carry on along the thorny and harsh path that leads to the longed-for heavenly country.

The number of churches, chapels, and sanctuaries that are dedicated to Mary is incalculable. They are found around the world in villages and deserts, mountains and valleys, and river banks and ocean beaches. Many countries are filled with simple and charming hermits who are dedicated to Mary, and there are renowned sanctuaries that offer the most splendid worship, that allow her to display her goodness more and be visited more frequently by the faithful.

Thanks to God, the people in these places of our diocese are privileged with these things. There is in our territory a sanctuary which contains the image of her as God's treasurer. The heavenly treasures are abundantly spread out there, and the faithful flock to these places and loudly proclaim, "Virgin of Las Lajas! You are the glory of Jerusalem! You are the joy of Israel! You are the honor of our people!"

If we attempt, my beloved faithful, to seek other words that we can put into your mouths to more faithfully express what the Virgin of Las Lajas is for you, it would be difficult to find others than those from the divine source of Holy Scripture. For other places, other words could be selected from this arsenal of beauty, Sacred Scripture. However, for the people of this diocese we do not know any better than these already spoken, which are words that respond to a truth found in everyone's consciences. The security of these words is like the soul of devotion of these people, and their certainty is for them like an axiom.

The Virgin of Las Lajas is the glory of the people of this region. She calls the faithful from faraway lands with her goodness. The faithful hear this eloquent voice of deeds. They come to her sanctuary. They experience her good deeds and return to their towns, where they preach how happy this region is because it possesses this precious joy, which is the most beautiful jewel and true glory.

This precious testimony from foreigners is of great value. But for us, beloved faithful, it is not necessary because from their earliest childhood the locals hear from their parents, who heard it from their parents of her titles of glory of this Catholic region. You and they have heard this special title of glory: "The Virgin of Las Lajas." In addition, they came and felt it.

What is the history of the Virgin of Las Lajas? We asked and searched for relics, but the only reply was, "We had them, but sacrilegious hands took them. Some of them ended up with a known person who confessed to having them, though we don't know how. Until today, no one has reported anything useful and beneficial."

We have found no history, but an abundance of glory for this region. We have found no written history to tell us of the miracles of goodness of the venerated image of Las Lajas. But we have found a beautiful history indelibly recorded in the hearts of the faithful. Yes, each heart of the good faithful is a poetic and eloquent page of this history. Each heart consists of innumerable blessings that Our Lady de Las Lajas has poured out. Each heart consists of the glory that this has given to this region. No sacrilegious hands can snatch away this glorious history. It exists, and will exist, despite men's impiety. It will always attest that Our Lady of Las Lajas is an inexhaustible source of goodness and glory for these people, who with good reason can say: "Virgin of Las Lajas, You are our glory: *Tu gloria Jerusalem!*"

The Virgin of Las Lajas is also the joy of these people: *Tu laetitia Israel.*

The fruit of bastardly passions and repugnant vices is a foolish, crazy, harmful, and evil joy. It brings weariness and is the sister of pain and door of mourning, as the wise teach us. The joy of the Virgin of Las Lajas is not and cannot be this joy. The joy of the Virgin for these people is an innocent and consoling joy.

Ask those who flock to the throne of graces that Our Lady has established in Las Lajas if what I say is true, and they will immediately respond: "Nothing is comparable to the innocent joy that the Virgin of Las Lajas infuses. She knows how to speak of our souls by appealing to our feelings. She opens the way to the most intimate parts of our hearts. She penetrates, recreates, and sweetly charms them. In her presence, the old are rejuvenated when they request her blessings on their descendants. The child leaps for joy and claps and rejoices. The fully content mother brings her children as close as possible to see the Virgin, and the children are thereby satisfied. The young Christian lady feels the joy of a chaste heart, which is the most sublime and heavenly thing. The young man experiences joys that he does not encounter in worldly pleasures. The poor sinner experiences the inexpressible joy that gives hope for forgiveness. The righteous sees the joy that is given for a good conscience. The suffering encounters the joy that causes the cure of hardships or at least the soothing from Christian acceptance. All find pure, holy, innocent joy, as the Virgin who inspires us and whom we adore is saintly, pure, and innocent."

You only have to seek outside of yourselves, beloved faithful, the proof of what has been said. You give such proof abundantly. With what joy in our heart do we hear the talk of Our Lady of Las Lajas! With what pleasure do we see your journeys to her Sanctuary to visit her! There we see the bestowal of her mercies, and testimonials of your gratitude. No, you are not giving in to a sterile devotion that is without foundation. You are not putting your confidence in a doubtful or chimerical power, as a known and blasphemous heretic said in some places, and who had to flee because he did not dare to fight with an entire region which would have oppressed him under the weight of such a sweet and consoling truth. No, a thousand times no. The years witness to the fact that your confidence is not misguided. Your faith is not mocked. Stimulated from this confidence, faith, and experience, let us praise the Virgin, glorify her, and say: You, oh Virgin of Las Lajas! You will be our joy. *Tu laetitia Israel.*

If the Virgin of Las Lajas is the glory and joy of these people, how is it that she is not also their honor? She is. To convince us of her we can go to her sanctuary and observe what occurs there. We will see that she is the honor of all of humanity and even of the angelic choirs themselves. In this picturesque location, in a special manner, her power and her goodness are clearly given in this manner to these people. This is therefore a special honor that is not given to others who lack such a renowned sanctuary.

When nations and individuals have honor, this comes from the goodness of he who guides them towards her. If their pride pushes them to leave, they repeat the frightening and abominable *non serviam* of the father of pride. True honor comes from God. He sends it. To the people to whom he sends his mother so that her goodness manifests in a special way, he gives a special honor that is more significant than every human honor. It is the most valuable gift, and provides every material advancement possible.

Who among you would suggest for the people of this region a greater honor than having Our Lady of Las Lajas? Search, if you want, an honor that outshines this honor...There is not one, you will not find one, nor would you want one for your people. Every other honor is poor, stingy, and small compared to this. We have the Virgin of Las Lajas, and with her the glory, the joy, and honor of our people. *Tu gloria Jerusalem, tu laetitia Israel, tu honorificentia populi nostri.*

I leave your souls the sweet task of meditating on what I have said. You will be obliged to confess and preach the preference with which you see the sublime mother of God, the mercies that distinguish her, and the blessings that she showers on you. Do then, with her, what Bethulia did with Judith, who is her figure. Praise and bless her, and give her as much glory as you can. Make your recognition public. Make an effort to honor her. Now is the time.

The sanctuary of Our Lady of Las Lajas, so picturesque and devout, is on many occasions too small, as you know, to welcome all the faithful who flock there to demonstrate their devotion and love for the Queen of Heaven. Therefore, we plan to build a large and beautiful church for Our Lady. But where? In the air, if I could express myself so. The present sanctuary, as you know, is set into the mountain, with the deep channel of the Guátara on the opposite side. At this point, the place is called Carchi. It is not possible to enlarge the church either from the back or sides. It is therefore necessary to build a church in front of the present sanctuary, where there is now only air between the two above-mentioned mountains and over the river, which flows far below.

How can this great and bold work be carried out? With the help of Our Lady of Las Lajas. She inspired the project and will provide the means. Some have expressed a lack of confidence. But the Virgin is powerful, and confident of her power, and has already given the start to the work. Everything is being enthusiastically prepared, and with God's help on September 15, the principal feast day of Our Lady of Las Lajas, we will have the great pleasure of laying the foundation stone with all the solemnity that the occasion demands and that the Pontifical requires.

Devotees of Our Lady of Las Lajas! Now is the time, I repeat, to give public testimony of your recognition of the goodness of the Virgin, and to demonstrate that She is indeed your glory, joy, and honor. From this moment, the Holy Virgin extends her hand to receive the offerings for her church until completion. The numerous offerings to Our Lady are particularly special on her feast day. Those who cannot visit her on this day can demand a memento from their family members or friends who come. Let there be no single believer in the whole region who does not contribute to or participate in some way to the church of the divine Lady. Happy are those who see the great sanctuary of Our Lady of Las Lajas completed and who can say, "I took part in this church. I gave alms to make it. I contributed with my labor to build it. I carried limestone, sand, and wood. I prayed to heaven so that it would be built . . . because it was the only way that I could contribute."

In order to help in the construction of this church, we order that every parish in the diocese take a collection on each of the principal feasts of Our Lady, that is, the Days of Purification, Annunciation, Ascension, Birth, and Conception for the entire duration of the construction of the church.

Holy Virgin of Las Lajas! Our beloved Mother! You are the charm of these places. They do not want to live without you, nor seek a greater honor than what you possess. Oh, loving Virgin! May you fulfill our desire to build the church so that on your feast days your devoted followers do not have to be outside of your house, where the functions that are celebrated in order to give you glory of splendor and magnificence take place. Bless our projects, and with your power bring them to completion. Stretch out your blessed hands over this region, which is your inheritance, and send the sweet dew of your mercy, so that we are content with worship and devotion to you in this life. Let us work in a way that we will be able to keep you company and praise you in the other, greater happiness of heaven.

This pastoral letter will be read in all of the churches of our diocese on the first Sunday or feast day immediately after its reception.

Given in Pasto, on the feast day of
Nuestra Señora de las Nieves, August 5, 1899.
✛ Fr. Ezequiel, *Bishop of Pasto.*

ELEVENTH
Pastoral Letter

To the venerable clergy and faithful of our Diocese, greetings and blessings in our Lord Jesus Christ.

W E GLADLY FULFILL THE DUTY of remembering, beloved children, that the sacred time is already near in which the Church, our Mother, takes on the forty days of mourning. She preaches fasting and penance to her sons. She makes the mournful laments of the prophets heard. She celebrates the most august mysteries of our religion and shares the abundant treasures of divine clemency. She places before men, who are forgetful of their salvation, all the most timely and conducive means to their entering the paths of truth and duty. What affectionate appeals to her sons does this good mother make in the holy time of Lent, whose approach we announce! How important it is to listen to her in these times! May God in his goodness move these voices of order, peace, and love to end the canon blasts and noise of weapons! Good heavens, put on your mourning. Cover your faces, angels of peace. Passionately loving seraphim, burst forth in sad tears. All of heaven's inhabitants, let us lament our misfortunes and beg the Eternal King of all creatures for a remedy!

We are at war. It is the cause of tears, orphans, and destruction. Human blood flows in torrents and soaks the earth. Thousands of cadavers are food for birds of prey and carnivorous animals. Souls that have been redeemed with the blood of the Immaculate Heart sink from the battlefield to the depths of hell to continue from there the terrible task of eternally blaspheming the Sacred Name of God. Lucifer cries out again, *non serviam, I will not serve. Long live liberty!* His imitators, the liberals, follow in letting out the same heinous cry, mixing with it the cry, *"Die Christ!"* and other truly horrific things. My God, what misfortune, what iniquity! There are even those who are part of this gang that imitates and follows Lucifer who call themselves Catholic! There are even Catholics who express their compliance with these doctrines and even with the methods of this sect, which is the enemy of God and his Christ. Oh, how much guilt do these latter have for the misfortunes that we suffer!

The present war has taken hold of everyone's attention. It is in everyone's thoughts, and preoccupies everyone. Given this, we are going to make sure that this preoccupation be Catholic or that people think in the Catholic way with respect to the present war, so that holy fruit comes from it. That is the goal of this pastoral letter, and let us pray that we achieve this.

I

What is the present war, from a Catholic perspective? This is the first question that we need to ask in order to achieve the object that we proposed.

To be on more certain ground with such questions, it is important that we not stray from the teachings of our holy mother Church. Then we can be sure of avoiding errors. What, then, does the Church teach on this matter or question? She has always seen public calamities as a *punishment from God*. We therefore conclusively teach this to organize the way and means of requesting forgiveness from God on such occasions. Scripture offers us abundant testimony to support the same truth. The Holy Fathers and Doctors of the Church speak in the same sense, and the Christian peoples, thus instructed, have no other explanation for public calamities, except that they are *punishments from God*.

The present war is therefore a punishment from God, in the Catholic sense of things, or what is the same: Our Lord God permits the war that is afflicting us at the moment, punishing us with this permission.

God does nothing nor can do nothing without proposing a goal in what he does. It is the nature of every intelligent and free being to always have a goal in his operations. This is the nature of God, who is infinite intelligence and is a free being by essence. God's goal in permitting the present war is, as already stated, to punish us. But is this the only and ultimate end? No, this end is subordinated to superior ends that constitute the ultimate and true end.

The *Catechism*, a small book of great substance that we learned and memorized from childhood and that many, unfortunately, forget, teaches us that man was created in order to love and serve God in this life, and then to behold and enjoy him in eternity. This is man's ultimate end: To behold and enjoy him for eternity. God directs and prepares all events of this world in view of this end. In this way, if man follows God's way, everything will help him to achieve his ultimate and happy end. Punishment itself admirably serves to the achievement of this end, when it is received in a proper way and according to divine ordination.

Only with a punishment does God aim to punish, and exclusively punish. With the punishment of hell he imposes his justice on the man who dies in mortal sin, that is, deprived of his friendship and grace. This is the sole punishment that can be strictly known as such. With it God does not propose any ultimate ends of mercy. With other punishments, God does not propose only to punish, but to warn the guilty one, call him to repentance, and seek his eternal salvation with this temporary punishment. But the punishment of hell does not involve these ends, and that is why it is eternal. This punishment is exclusive and is the most tremendous work of divine justice. God works in this punishment solely as Judge. In the others, He also acts as Father.

The punishment of this war is therefore not the ultimate end, as this end only involves divine justice. We can conclude from what is said that this punishment involves further goals of mercy. It is a warning, a calling to repentance, and, in a word, an act for our good and eternal salvation if we use it for this. Punishment is still punishment, and supposes guilt. When it is considered in this sense, the following question presents itself naturally and without intellectual effort: "What sin brought on this great punishment for the nation?" Let us answer this question without qualms or fears as our duty. We have no other intention than to put into view certain sins so as to correct them and so we can throw ourselves into the arms of God.

II

In the afterlife, men expect a rigorous judgment which will give an exact account of all their works. They will be sentenced and condemned to the punishments that correspond with their crimes, if they die without repenting of them in a way that obtains pardon for them. Societies cannot expect such judgment, and for this, when they sin, they are punished in this same life with collective punishment for their sins. The Church Fathers and Doctors have taught this doctrine. It has been repeated by preachers of the divine word and believed by Christian peoples because it is supported, as well, in the Bible.

The nation is receiving a punishment, and a very large punishment, which is war. What sins of the nation have brought on this great punishment? As noted, we will point this out without fear or qualms, and only with the goal of correction. We will give the main principles that appear to relate to this.

No one can deny that there is much publicly-known cohabitation. There is hardly a single town that does not have such disgraceful scandals, and not a small number either. What makes this serious situation worse is that, despite the commitment from zealous and concerned people to take this to the authorities, no one has sought a remedy. The reason is unknown, but it is certain that in the majority of these cases that were brought before the judges, the delinquents were triumphant and laughed at the plaintiffs. My priests have told me much about trying to deal with scandals in these places. We have also personally observed this.

Drunkenness is another public sin, and very common. It also merits public and collective punishment.

The sins of the press—who can count them? Through the press, God, his Most Holy Son, his ministers and morality have been insulted. Here (I do not know of other areas), these all are not only left unpunished, but also on one occasion we respectfully raised a complaint with the superior judge, supported by the law that as bishop the laws grant us over the material government of the republic, and we received no acknowledgement of receipt. This slap in the face did not fall on us. It was given to the divine face of Our Lord Jesus Christ, whom liberalism ridicules and blasphemes through a newspaper, in which the writers follow what the directors think. God is just, and now punishes us with the same forbearance that he had when his Divine Majesty was offended.

If there was leniency in allowing insults, such as those pointed out, to be published, it was no less important to let the most impious and filthy writings into the country. The border areas of this diocese were inundated with this type of corrupting and disgusting trashy writing, the work of the masons and liberals of Ecuador. How much has that trashy writing stoked the fire of the present rebellion? And who bears the guilt?

In teaching, many sins are also committed that cry to heaven because they are against children, who are so loved by the Divine Savior. In one area of this bishopric, all of the school teachers were liberals except for only one or two. Parish priests claim this, lamenting this great scandal, about which they can do nothing.

It is well known that in Bogotá itself there are teaching centers that are nothing other than seedbeds of heresy and impiety. The *Universidad Republicana* is one of these centers. Its name recalls to us a sad event, a great sin on the part of old dignitaries whom we have mentioned in order to reproach them and avoid harm to our diocese. We sometimes need the courage reflected in the words of the royal prophet: *Loquebar de testimoniis tuis in conspectu regum et non confundebar.*[1] If we bishops do not condemn these sins, who will correct the evil, or at least point out how to identify and avoid it?

The scandalous event to which we refer is the following: On last September 21 in Bogotá, Dr. Luis A. Robles

---

1 "And I spoke of thy testimonies before kings: and I was not ashamed" (Ps. 118:46).

died. He was the rector of the seedbed of heresies, of which I previously mentioned, that is, the Universidad Republicana. This rector brought his followers to shout their opposition to the master's body being taken to the church. Dr. Robles, then, developed his students' impiety with his teachings, and was for some time recognized as one of the most distinguished leaders of liberalism in Colombia. This man was an enemy of Jesus Christ who stole souls from God and trained impious students. The consequence of his actions was, in his giving revolutionaries to the nation, that the nation's government, as a revolutionary government, paid tribute to those who were elected. This was given in decree number 429, dated September 22, 1899. This decree has one article, which declares: "The government mourns the death of Dr. Luis A. Robles, and considers the absence of this illustrious citizen as an unfortunate event for the Republic."

We cannot express the profound pain that reading this article caused us. How!? A Catholic government *mourns* the death of an enemy of God, a propagandist of heresies, an agent of hell who perverted and condemned souls? How!? A Catholic government dares to say that it considers this man's death *an unfortunate event* for the republic? This all seems like a dream, but the kind of dream that frightens and menaces. We want to suppose—and we eagerly do so—that the government does not have any bad intentions by giving this decree. But even so, one can see the sad and terrifying consequences of these leading thinkers of the nation, perhaps without realizing it. This comes from their drinking the poison of error, and thereby going so far as to call good bad, and bad good, light darkness, and darkness light. There is nothing else, then, but to judge an enlightened citizen as an enemy of God and propagator of impiety when he considers this death to be *an unfortunate event* for the republic. It is necessary to condemn such an erroneous way of thinking, because coming as it does from such high levels, it could be imitated.

We have left some sins unstated because the sins that we already mentioned suffice for the present objective. All these sins brought the nation the punishment of war that we are now suffering. Having complied with error and with God's enemies, God permits those same enemies to punish us. We pray to his Divine Majesty that we learn from the punishment!

We cannot end this point without making the following clarification: Our objection to the government's error may lead some less well-read individuals to conclude that we do not support the government. We must therefore declare that if we have disapproved of this fault, it is only so that it can be corrected, just as with other cases of tolerance of evil. This does not mean that we do not support the government. We support it with all of our powers, and urge everyone, with all our heart and in the name of God, to support and defend it because it is the legitimate government and represents order in opposition to an anti-religious and antisocial revolution.

We will now show how this punishment includes a great mercy, as I have already indicated.

III

Once the error was admitted in and treated so kindly, as I just mentioned, it extended its sphere of action and actively propagated its ideals. Soon we were surrounded everywhere by an atmosphere of liberalism. The destructive nature of this plague was visible. Some died totally due to their lives of faith. Others were affected by terrible evil. Still others wanted truth and error to embrace and walk together. Not a few, perhaps unconsciously, favored the spread of these evils and became accomplices and aids.

We were walking towards an abyss, and God permitted the cannon's boom to warn us before we fell in.

God, the Almighty and infinite good, does not want, nor could want, sin. But having given man free will, he respects man's free action to the point at which man suffers from sin. This is the abuse of free will that God gave, and he bears this until the time comes when he enacts punishment. As long as this time has not yet arrived, and he permits it, he finds in his boundless wisdom admirable means to draw good from evil. He uses these means to contribute to the well-being and glorification of those who love him.

The present war, then, permits the Lord to produce great goods. He is doing just this. We only have to watch a little of what is happening to see and understand what we are saying.

We have outlined the havoc that liberalism was doing to souls with its periodicals, brochures, addresses, propaganda, and with the ill-fated and guilty deference that we encountered. Who did not clearly observe how suddenly the healthy and rightful aversion that one should have towards liberal ideas was sparked? Who did or does not see this ardor which grew into a heat in the Catholic breast that defends healthy principles, even at the cost of Catholics' own blood and own lives? Who does not happily see the countless hearts beating to the impulses of the most delicate religious sentiments which are reflected in tender and moving words and deeds for Christian heroism and living faith? Oh! How many mothers encouraged their sons to go to the war to defend religion even when they feared they would not see them again! How many wives carried the whole weight of the house and worked to feed the family so that their husbands could march to the defense of the good cause! How many sisters hang the scapular of the Virgin around the neck of their brothers, and encourage and excite them to fight for Jesus Christ! How many valiant men voluntarily enlist in the ranks of the government troops, all moved by the same religious motive! How many sublime elements of faith and Christian heroism were present in the battle camps! Blessed be God, who takes so much glory for himself and so much good for souls from such a great evil as war!

To these preceding elements, that we can call heroic, we can add thousands and thousands of pious acts done for the faithful in view of the war. Many among us—blessed be God!—have not ceased to pray, receive the sacraments, and carry out other religious acts. Novenas to Nuestra Señora de las Mercedes have followed one after the other, and her processions through the streets of this city have been truly triumphant. Blessed Virgin, delight of your children and distinguished protectress of your people! Do not permit those who confess, adore, and love you to become the prey of your enemies!

Our Lord God will be pleased to see how virtue has reached a heroic level in certain souls that, without the shock of this war, would have given in to laziness and indifference as regards to religion, or would have lay prostrate from lethargy caused by the poison of the error that they were taking in without thought or notice. Without this spark that the Lord permitted, we would not have seen so much heroism or so many fervent acts of piety.

Each round from the enemies of the faith awoke hundreds of brave Christian soldiers who were moved to defend and confess this faith. Women themselves have become warriors in great numbers. Moved by the religious spirit, they have found strength from their weakness, and do amazing deeds. Above all, they pray—and pray often and with a truly Christian fervor. We owe our triumphs primarily to them. We all believe and confess, and the same courageous soldiers confess in the letters that they write from the camps that they are palpably seeing divine protection. If it is true that prayer leads to divine protection, it is undoubtedly women who are responsible for the greatest part of the triumphs through their edifying and touching way of praying. Courageous soldiers of the cause of religion and order! You can be satisfied with the conduct of your mothers, spouses, brothers, and other relations because they have followed you in all things in the divine presence with their prayers, hearts, and tears. They have therefore placed you under Our Lady's loving mantle so that she can shelter and protect you.

IV

If the calamity of the war that afflicts us is a punishment from God, brought on by our sins, and if this punishment involves God's mercy because it is a warning that calls and rouses us to reject evil and do good, what must we therefore do? This is the question that we will now discuss. It is obvious that this is a practical question.

The first thing that we must do is lower our heads before the Just and Omnipotent God, whom we have offended and who punishes us. We must confess our sins and ask for forgiveness. Woe to the peoples and individuals who do not do penance despite such formidable warning about the anger of God! In this case, heaven's punishment will only serve to further harden the unfortunate who are punished and to worsen their miserable and sad states. They will no longer be able to rise from these states except by a miracle of divine mercy. We must, then, confess before God that we have sinned, sincerely repent of the sin, and humbly ask for forgiveness.

We are all more or less responsible for the evils afflicting our nation. All have been more or less complicit, even if not the true authors of the sins that provoked God's wrath. Some sins involve what we have said or done while others what we have not said or done when we were able and this was required. More than a few sins involve the much good that could have been done to counter these evils but was not done. Therefore, there is hardly anyone who does not have some responsibility, and who consequently does not need to repent and ask God for forgiveness.

But it is not enough to repent and ask for forgiveness if we do not strongly attempt to better ourselves and avoid acting as before. Whoever continues to commit the same sins as before and lives the same life as before is not repenting. If we are still lenient towards heresy and error in Colombia, and even praise those who profess and propagate these; if we continue to allow the unmarried to live together and other sins that we can stop; and if we continue to publicly offend God, we will have not repented. Then God will bring justice to the community that is responsible for having provoked him, just as he does with the individual who comes to the hour of judgment without having repented.

The great sin of our time for many self-declared Catholics is the indifference with which they look on the offenses that are committed against Our Lord God and how these offenses seem so normal and natural that they are permitted without anyone taking any corrective actions. These people think of themselves as Catholic only because they do not persecute religion or mistreat priests. Apart from that, they are indifferent as to whether worship takes place or not, God is adored or not, and God offended or not. They belong to this class of *honorable gentlemen* who do not mess with anyone, as they themselves say. They have an affectionate smile for religion, and accommodating smiles for its enemies. They speak the language of the faithful disciples of Jesus Christ when among them, and the language of the emulators of

Lucifer when needing their services. They do not see, or do not want to see, how repugnant this conduct is. In their blindness, they go so far as to believe that they are *prudent* in addition to honorable. Guided by this same criteria, they judge as imprudent and intolerant those who proclaim the whole and plain truth or those who speak out against scandals and offenses which are committed against morality, religion, and God. Unfortunately, there are many such men of this type among the enlightened and well-to-do. When they get into positions of power, they are a true calamity. Their tolerance and leniency towards error and vice are responsible for great evils.

We must, then, repent and try to avoid offenses against His Divine Majesty so that he withdraws his punishment and offers us his protection. Colombians allow sins either for the gratification of men or out of fear of them, and fail to consider that the more sins are permitted, the more God removes his protection. This abandons us even more to the enemy, whom we have tried to make content despite how much this displeases God. Conversely, if we avoid offenses against God, he shows gratitude and blesses the peoples and individuals who give him glory in this way. He protects them and humbles their enemies.

V

Once we have sincerely repented of our sins, with the firm intention of not committing them again, we can already confidently move closer to God, and ask that he move away from us or end the calamity that afflicts us. Continuing the same offense while daring to request the cessation of its effects would clearly be insolence, which is worthy of a major punishment.

Let us all make requests, as the souls have been continually doing, through novenas, frequent reception of sacraments, general communions, rosaries, and whatever else piety has to offer, including promises and almsgiving. Associations should celebrate special functions to honor their patrons and pray in common with more fervor than usual. Good souls have a more intimate relationship with God. They are more favored by him and are therefore more ready for sacrifice and self-offering. They will extend this self-offering as much as possible in support of their brothers and make amends to God and give him glory. They will go as far as the heroism of offering themselves as expiatory sacrifices. They are prepared by the grace of God to offer whatever he wants, including who they are and what they have, up to their very lives. Oh, how much can these souls achieve, and how much must they do, so that they receive more light to know, the worth of souls, the horror, fear of eternal perdition, what Our Lord God deserves, and how pleasing this is to Jesus Christ, who is the sacrifice who did this to save us! Our lovable Redeemer Jesus was the first to offer himself to die for the salvation of everyone. Since then, following his example, an infinite number of just souls have offered their lives for the same holy end. God's Church never lacks these generous souls who are prepared for every kind of sacrifice for the good of their neighbors. We are sure that in the present circumstances we will not lack souls to make the generous offer of their own lives for the good of their brothers. We are sure that these hidden sacrifices have succeeded and have obtained invaluable goods from God.

Each should do what he can to appease God's anger and obtain mercy. If the revolution triumphs, the Church, souls, people, and families will face a terrifying fate. No one is ignorant of what liberalism is and what it seeks because it has clearly shown this. A faithful servant of masonry, it makes war against God, the Church, and every good. It does this through impious and coarse journalism, atheistic laws that endorse error and vice, the profanation of churches and altars and the plundering of sacred and private homes, offenses against morals and decency, and the establishment of the right to corrupt and be corrupted.

If liberalism wages war against God, it is the duty of each Catholic to fight with all his strength. We have the infallible certainty of victory, because man can fight God, but cannot defeat him. With him we will be victorious even when everyone falls on the battlefield. Let us fight, then, with determination, each one where he is and with his own weapons. Those at home can pray unceasingly and fervently for the courageous ones who are in the camps.

Let everyone strive to be in the grace and love of God, and do everything and face every suffering for his love and his service. Let us all strive to remember that even if hell bellows in fury, it is an eternal truth that Christ is victorious and prevails. May Christ rule from now over all the nations, families, and individuals. Your bishop desires that Christ sanctify and bless you all, and he also blesses you in the name of the Father ✠ and of the Son ✠ and of the Holy Spirit ✠. Amen.

> Given and signed from Us, and stamped
> with our seal and endorsed by our
> secretary in Pasto, on the Feast of the
> virgin St. Scholastica, on February 10, 1900.
> ✠ Fr. Ezequiel, *Bishop of Pasto.* Sent by
> Reverend Anselmo Guerrero, secretary.

FOURTEENTH
Pastoral Letter

ON THE OCCASION OF LENT, 1902.
IN THE LETTER, THE BISHOP OF
PASTO DISCUSSES THE UNITY THAT
MUST EXIST AMONG CATHOLICS,
AND HOW AND WHY THIS
SHOULD BE ACHIEVED.

To the reverend clergy and faithful of our diocese: greetings and blessings in our Lord Jesus Christ.

IF WE HAD NO OTHER PROOF OF THE loving eagerness of our holy mother Church for our eternal salvation, the institution of Holy Lent would by itself be the most eloquent testimony of this truth. How many ways of sanctification are given us in this time! How many calls to the heart of man through its rites, commandments, and preachers!

In order to hear these calls from the Church and benefit from the means of sanctification that Holy Lent offers us, it is necessary to abstain completely from worldly distractions in this time. The soul fills with mourning, just as the Church wears it with its vestments. We strive for interior recollection, and continually preoccupy ourselves with grave thoughts on the soul, including death, judgment, hell, glory, eternity.

This is the practice of truly Catholic peoples. The majestic and stunning ceremonies of the Church, which impress and move the soul, are crowded. Attendance for sermons is high, attentive, and reflective. The spiritual fruit from Lent is abundant and consoling.

We can observe the contrary in peoples who regard the time of Holy Lent as any other in the year. The people are devoted to ordinary and profane distractions and do no practice whatsoever of interior recollection. They do not hear the call of the Church, or take advantage of the abundant means of sanctification that are offered. But woe to those peoples who do not observe Holy Lent!

The wise Pope Benedict XIV, speaking of this point, declares the following: "The observation of Lent is the link to our hosts. Through this observation, we distinguish ourselves from the enemies of the Cross of Jesus Christ. Through this time of penitence we stop the penalties and scourges of divine justice. A failure or weak observance of Lent lessens the glory of God, dishonors the Catholic religion, and endangers Christian souls. We do not doubt for an instant that this negligence is the origin of great disasters for peoples and nations — countless disasters in the public interest, and fatal results for individuals" (Constitution *Non ambigimus*).

Let us, then, observe Holy Lent to avoid chastisements from divine justice and to be the link to our fighters, who distinguish us from the enemies of Christ's Cross. What is precisely needed at the present is to attain through the observation of Holy Lent, as regards our part, the beautiful thought that Our Lord Jesus Christ expressed in these words: "That they all may be one, as thou, Father, in me, and I in thee; that they also may be one in us; that the world may believe that thou hast sent me."[1] The first Christians fulfilled this thought of the Divine Redeemer according to Holy Scripture that says, "And the multitude of believers had but one heart and one soul."[2]

---

1   John 17:21.
2   Acts 4:32.

Let us also strive to achieve this sweet and beautiful union based on the same faith because this will placate God and bring us every kind of abundance. There are unpleasant and ruinous divisions for the cause of God and his Church. We will discuss the unity that is needed among Catholics, and how it must be achieved.

I

Jesus Christ came into the world
to re-establish with unity of men

Men should have been united from the beginning of the world because that is what the Creator wanted. He bestowed on every creature its own being with a certain independence from each other. But when it came to creating the human race, he created *a single* man from whom all others came so that, understanding that we are all brothers, we would live united like a single family.

This loving divine plan did not develop as God had intended. Abusing the liberty granted by God, men hated each other. They became divided and persecuted each other as enemies instead of living united and loving each other as brothers. God inscribed a law on the heart of each man from the first, and then later wrote it down for men on Sinai. Over this law of mutual love those same men wrote black blots of resentment, rivalry, and hatred.

The Divine Word had pity on humanity's deep divisions and the great evils that afflicted it. It was necessary for the Word to leave the throne of his glory and come down to earth to cure and unite humanity. He did this in his goodness. He took on our flesh and nature and carried out the marvelous work of saving man, achieving the sublime and loving mysteries that we recall in the holy time of Lent. With his humiliation, suffering, and precious death, Jesus Christ restored the reign of love and united men who were divided by egoism, vice, and sin. Jesus Christ died to bring together in one the sons of God who were dispersed. *Ut filios Dei qui erant dispersi congregaret in unum* (John 11:51).

For the same purpose of uniting men with his doctrine, Jesus Christ broke down the walls that divide people from people and men from men. He founded his holy Church so that all, without distinction, could enter it and enjoy its riches. He pointed the way to the same sublime and eternal destinies for everyone.

With this background, we are able to enter and better understand this sweet and touching request that the Divine Redeemer directs to the Eternal Father on Maundy Thursday, and in which he clearly explains his last will.

Four thousand years of divisions, hate, and revenge among men elapsed from creation to Jesus Christ. This gives us sufficient understanding that the unity for which the Divine Savior came to plead at that time was very difficult. Therefore, according to St. John, raising his eyes to heaven, he said: "Father, the hour is come, glorify thy Son, that thy Son may glorify thee."[3]

There is no doubt that the Son of God, who begins his prayer in this majestic and solemn tone, would ask for something greater: "Holy Father, keep them in thy name whom thou has given me; that they may be one, as we also are."[4] This was a prayer in favor of his disciples. Later in the same prayer he adds, "And not for them only do I pray, but for them also who through their word shall believe in me. That they all may be one, as thou, Father, in me, and I in thee; that they also may be one in us; that the world may believe that thou hast sent me."[5]

Can Jesus Christ express his desire in a more solemn and touching manner that all those who believe in him

---

3   John 17:1.
4   John 17:11.
5   John 17:20, 21.

be united? Since then, Jesus continues to desire this unity and seeks through every means of sanctification that he left to his Church. He takes care to propose to everyone the same truths, that is, the same faith. He gives to everyone the same hope in a blessed eternity. He orders everyone to do mutual charity. He imposes the same precepts. He gives joy to everyone with the same worship. He gives new life to everyone with the same sacraments, especially with the Holy Eucharist, through which he brings the unity of all men. Everyone is united in Jesus Christ by receiving Jesus Christ. This is what signifies *communion*, which is *communis unio*, common unity.

Unfortunately, nowadays we see men among us who are in agreement with the profession of faith, but who are nevertheless in conflict and disunity. They want the triumph of the cause of God, but they want this with certain people or only through means that they think are appropriate. They turn their weapons against those who do not think the same way. By doing so, they undo the plan of Jesus Christ and divide the body of this Divine Redeemer and tear it apart.

Let us bear in mind that it is Jesus Christ who requests unity, and that it is the distinguishing feature of his Church and true disciples. Following the teachings of his Divine Master, St. Paul also says to us, "Careful to keep the unity of the Spirit in the bond of peace."[6]

II

The disunity among the good is the work of Satan

If Jesus Christ came to unite men with the sweet bond of charity, the demon seeks to divide us through bitter hate. Every division among the good is caused by the evil spirit. This is the best means that he finds for ruining them.

---

6   Eph. 4:3.

There is no doubt that the works of division and dis-cord that we lament in the present day are the work of Satan, for in no other way can one explain the blindness of certain men who in other times provided evidence of good Christian sense. How can we explain people who demonstrated their adherence to Catholicism, and even defended it, and who were carried away by passions that are condemned by Catholicism? How can we understand so much aversion and enduring animosity among men who follow and profess the religion that mandates that we love even our enemies?

There are many things, through sacrifice, that can be done for the common good of the undertakings that unite us. How is it, then, great God, that certain men who boast of being Catholics do not make the sacrifice of self-love for the good of religion, the fatherland, the family, and themselves? Satan himself stirs the fire of discord. He helps endlessly prolong differences of opinion that could be resolved very quickly if we remember that the principal individuals responsible for these divisions have displayed their talent and wisdom for many years.

They do not want to yield to resolutions that have already been adopted, but focus on secondary questions that they could and must relinquish in favor of the fun-damental questions. Those who behave in this way must seriously reflect. They must come to see that those who concede to others and imagine everyone saying of them, "He gave in," do not in fact suffer in the least in the spirit of their character. On the contrary, they appear more powerful by voluntarily submitting to the moral force of the urgent demands of the public good. By acting this way and triumphing over themselves, which requires greater valor than defeating enemies on the battlefield, they give clear proof that their spirit of character is true, rational, and, above all, based on Catholic doctrine, and not on the blind movement of pride, capricious tenacity, or a stubborn and low passion that resists the laws of charity and justice, to get out of every such trance with this: "It is an honor for a man to separate himself from quarrels,"[7] declares the Holy Spirit.

It is the saddest thing to think that divisions can continue, and certain people—who can cause so much scandal—pay more attention to sensitivity, resentment, waning satisfaction from self-love, whim, and pride than they do to urgent calls for the common good and the voice of conscience. Let us say it again: All this would be the work of the devil, as we see in the following passage from St. James the Apostle: "But if you have bitter zeal, and there be contentions in your hearts; glory not, and be not liars against the truth. For this is not wisdom, descending from above: but earthly, sensual, devilish."[8]

If Satan works to divide the good, these individuals must lay aside every resentment for the good of religion and the fatherland. They must promote charity among themselves, and thereby follow the counsel of the apostle, who says: "Now I beseech you, brethren, by the name of our Lord Jesus Christ, that you all speak the same thing, and that there be no schisms among you; but that you be perfect in the same mind, and in the same judgment."[9] We can justly emphasize that religious sentiment has overcome the spirit of division in these parts.

III

The unity among the good was fought against and made necessary by the unity of Satan's sectarians

Satan is not unaware of the great power that comes from human unity and the prodigious results that its

---

7   Prov. 20:3.
8   James 3:14–15.
9   1 Cor. 1:10.

work brings about. Accordingly, while working to unite his own, he strives to divide the good so that they lack this power. Unfortunately, he has achieved this unity.

How did the devil achieve this unity of his own? What bond of unity can he give to his own sectarians? In fact, they do not have unity of faith since each one believes what he wants, or believes in nothing. They do not have unity in hope because they do not see heavenly reward. Each one seeks his own comfort as his aspiration. They are not connected by love because they are separated from God. They are not united in morality because each one understands this in his own way. Nevertheless, it is certain that these men have formed the tightest connection. How? Let us say it again: What bond does Satan use to maintain unity? The bond that he uses is hatred of Our Lord Jesus Christ and everything that belongs to him. In this they are in accordance; it is the link that unites them.

It is an undeniable fact that there exists a vast association that, instead of being hidden, is visible and quasi-official. It counts millions of members, who are all united in the oath to completely eradicate, if possible, or at least reduce, the reign of Jesus Christ on earth. This association was secret and hidden until a few years ago. It now appears and presents itself in public with known leaders, subordinates, and centers in all nations. It is the church of Satan, who has declared and wages war on the Church of Jesus Christ to the death. It aspires to triumph over it.

This association is called *freemasonry*. In its desire to destroy Jesus Christ and establish the reign of Satan on earth, it works with a surprising zeal and with results that would frighten the Church if there had not been the promise that hell would not prevail against it.

This association has already established governments that clearly work against Jesus Christ. There are others who do not take his sacred religion into account for anything, and still others who claim that Jesus Christ agrees with much or some of his enemies, or is content with what they do. Leo XIII clearly teaches all of this with these words: "In the space of a century and a half, the freemasons have achieved incredible progress. Using boldness and astuteness at the same time, they have invaded all levels of the social hierarchy, and have started to exercise in the heart of the modern states a power that is almost sovereign" (Encyclical *Humanum genus*).

What a powerful affirmation! All ranks of society have been invaded by this dark conspiracy against Jesus Christ. The master of the truth, the vicar of Christ, tells us this. We walk, then, among enemies, and have to carefully take this into account because where we least expect them to be, there they are, hidden and waging war against Jesus Christ, plotting against the order of things and creating connections to divide and wreck us.

It is good to warn that there are men who are not masons because their names are not in the registers of the masons. But they still profess and practice the doctrines of masonry, which are those of liberalism. The power of the lodges would not be so frightening if liberal advocates of masonry did not help them even though they themselves are not freemasons.

To tackle these partisans and successfully fight against them, it is necessary that we also unite, as they do. Just as they are united by their hatred for Jesus Christ, so an ardent love for the same Jesus Christ and a great desire to support and extend his reign over the earth unites us. This is in opposition to the desire of those who wish to extend the reign of Satan.

Let us unite, then, in Jesus Christ and for the glory of Jesus Christ. When united, each one of us will be strengthened with the force of the others. Unity marvelously multiplies power. With such power, we can take advantage of things that as individuals we could not. Jesus Christ himself grants unity to his Church. All those who seek to do something for her glory must possess unity.

IV

Who must unite?

We come to the most difficult but perhaps most important point in this instruction.

There is no doubt that this unity must only include Catholics, because in various documents the Holy Father recommends union among Catholics to better resist those who wage war against the Church. He declares in one of these documents, "In the midst of unbridled liberty of thought, and the wild and insidious war that is everywhere waged against the Church, it is absolutely necessary that Christians resist all of this, united as one in their forces with perfect harmony of will, so that they do not find themselves divided and thereby succumb to the cunning and violence of their enemies" (Encyclical *Cum multa*).

Those who wage war against the Church, whether they are called atheists, rationalists, masons, or liberals, cannot enter the union because the union that is called for is precisely against them or to resist them, as the Holy Father declares.

But is it only those who wage open war against religion who must be kept away? No, this applies to others as well. Those who do not sincerely repent and change their conduct cannot enter into the union of Catholics:

1. Liberal Catholics, of whom the Vicar of Christ has said that they are *a harmful plague; a true present calamity; more dangerous and disastrous than declared enemies*; and similar things.

2. Those who say: "To more easily attract dissidents to the Catholic truth, it is necessary that

the Church adapts to the civilization of a world that has reached greater advancement. It must give up its old rigor and demonstrate a conciliatory attitude in accordance with the needs and aspirations of modern peoples" (Fundamentals of *Americanism*, which was condemned by Leo XIII in his Apostolic Letter *Testem benevolentiae*).

3. Those who say that they are "neither impious nor fanatics." They define fanaticism as indulgences, frequency of receiving the sacraments, popular practices of piety, and so on.

4. Those who are dominated by a false spirit of reconciliation and who try to build bridges over the abyss that separates Catholicism from liberalism so that liberals and Catholics get mixed up and confused without liberals stopping being who they are.

5. Those who take unjust precautions against the papacy and are zealously suspicious of the bishops, clergy, and religious orders. They become known for this with their politics, as they continually try to paralyze or lessen the influence of the Catholic clergy and religious institutions on the people. They have a certain repugnance for the participation of church leaders in the assemblies of the nation.

6. Those who in their conduct are constant accomplices of liberalism and justify this through unfounded pretexts.

While other examples could be added, we believe that they are included in what has been written. We end the list by stating that it would be dangerous to unite with this class of men, even though they call themselves Catholics, as long as they do not convert to God. These men, when among true Catholics, would do nothing more than discourage, weaken, divide, render the common power useless, and facilitate the triumph of the enemy.

V

Goals of the union

The union is not a simple association of people to achieve desired goals. The union must be based upon real unity, which consists in the same feeling, thinking, and desiring of those who enter the union. Due to this, everyone who does not feel, think, or desire in the same way as those in the union will be kicked out.

But how should true Catholics feel, think, and desire? To what ends must they be united? Catholics should be united to defend the rights of Jesus Christ and his Church in all regions that demand justice, and especially in the political-religious terrain.

The enemies of Jesus Christ desire that the nations get rid of him and take away his rights to social organization. The various types of liberalism are only various ways, more or less accentuated, to remove the rights of Jesus Christ from society. Absolute liberalism is the absolute suppression of these rights.

These enemies strive to secularize the state, legislation, teaching, religion, morality, holidays, welfare, marriage, birth, death itself, and even the grave. In everything and by everything they seek to separate from Jesus Christ and his religion.

These objectives of the enemies of Jesus Christ reveal what Catholics need to do. They need to support the rights of Jesus Christ where these are still recognized, and restore these rights where they have been violated. They need to fight against all political-religious errors, which have caused so much damage to the Church and society to the point of destroying individuals. They have to work to end the empire of liberalism and bring about the absolute reign of Jesus Christ in a way that honors him in the temple and the home, in private and public life, in the tribunals of justice and legislative chambers, in the agreements of local communities and the decrees of the central authorities.

Today, the revolution chose the field of battle for the fight. In this field, good Catholics must also fight united, keeping watch lest false brothers, who serve the enemy and bring about his triumph, enter the troop ranks.

When the present war ends, Catholics must remain united and work to elect municipal representatives who totally embrace the faith and customs, to send true and upright Catholics with clear consciences to the legislative assemblies and chambers. These representatives must be united in their actions to purify the laws from the errors that corrupt them, and to provide a genuinely Catholic spirit.

To do all the above is not a little task. Our laws have been praised many times for being very Catholic. But it is clear that there is liberty of worship. Besides churches and altars consecrated to the true God, the erection of buildings destined to blaspheme and insult those churches and altars is authorized and protected. There are schools where the faith that is learned in the houses of the fathers is torn out of the heart of the young. Civil marriage is allowed and has caused no shortage of scandals when certain Catholics want to get married in this way sometimes only to spite the priest. The expression of individual opinions on religion is allowed and protected, that is, freedom of conscience. These religious opinions, which are not Catholic, are errors and heresies. Books and brochures, riddled with heresies and filth, proliferate everywhere without any action from the authorities. A law still stands that excludes bishops and priests from the councils of the nation. This is directly for possessing special knowledge about the needs of the people and for sharing in these councils their special qualities and titles to serve for the benefit of the country. This exception is unjust, scornful of the clergy, and damaging of the people and nation.

How much would a congress, composed of true and pure Catholics, do to benefit Catholicism by dealing with the indicated materials and other such things with clearly Catholic criteria? Oh! Perhaps — or more certain than perhaps — must we now pay for the fact that we did not do as much good in this sense than we could have done if all of the representatives of the nation in the various legislatures had really been Catholic. Not only did they not reform certain laws as was necessary, but they also did not dare to dedicate the republic to the Sacred Heart of Jesus despite the people's petitioning for this. The fact that the Heart of God was rejected by the representatives of the nation was made worse because these representatives called themselves Catholics. Since then we have revealed our fear of punishment. Let us hope that in these crucial days, when we are called to make this consecration, we do so as soon as possible as a reparation of the past slight, as an apology, as a powerful way to appease the Divine Heart and remove from us the punishments from which we suffer!

In his goodness, this loving Heart wishes that we learn this lesson and take advantage of it. When we do not take advantage of such lessons, the people will inevitably die, and they are.

VI

Conclusion

The more that a nation gives to God, the more it obliges God to watch over, care for, and defend it. If, out of a false understanding of human considerations, the representatives of the nation do not take care to give him glory, they give him the motivation to withdraw his special protection with which he cares for it. St. Paul declares, "For the wisdom of the flesh is death; but the wisdom of the spirit is life and peace."[10]

Many think it is prudent to acquiesce to the demands of the enemies of Jesus Christ. However, the disastrous results that we have encountered demonstrate this to be prudence of the flesh, which is death. We are surrounded by dangers, and new torments threaten us. The enemies of religion and the country do not cease in their determination to ruin everything. They multiply their attacks, not only on the battlefield, but also in the field of ideas and customs in order to bring erroneous understanding and vice to the heart.

We must wrest away from apostasy as many as we can, and—oh! what misfortune!—we witness sad retreat, even among those who appear to be strongly grounded in the truth. Some have their faith totally destroyed, or accept one or many errors that are condemned by the Church. Others praise, even officially, known liberal leaders and disseminators of impiety. The former build bridges so that they can unite Catholics and liberals arm in arm. The disseminators ask that we reach agreement with the liberal leaders.

At present, a printed discourse is circulating that is attributed to a man full of hope. He praises a group of people that professes and practices all the religions. He claims that the Quran made conquests for civilization, and that if in the past the Cross was the civilizing force, now it is the Quran that is the powerful locomotive that awakens the people to progress, well-being, liberty, and civilization.

If all of this is true, then the pillar of this conservative group has also fallen, or at least been eaten through by

---

10   Rom. 8:6.

liberal termites. This is also true for the writer of a conservative periodical who, reporting on a speaking engagement, called it a *magnificent discourse* that, in spite of such assertions that are so contrary to the Catholic spirit.

We have various clippings from other conservative periodicals from this time that prove that the editors were infected by the terrible liberal plague, and that as a consequence they also conformed to liberalism with their writings. No one should be surprised, then, over what happened because many were already affected by the terrible evil.

We can see the symptoms that announce our path towards a dreadful catastrophe. This will come to pass if good, united Catholics do not make an effort to stop it. Everyone must unite, then, with those who remained standing in the middle of this decline and did not kneel before the heinous idol known as *liberalism*. We must unite with those who did not let themselves be seduced through sophistry, illusions, or examples that enrapture, and who are firm in their beliefs. They steadfastly lift the beautiful and clean banner of Catholicism that is without the smallest stain of liberal error, and display it in front of the enemy, determined to defend it at the cost of their blood and lives. Clearly, Catholics must unite, but only those Catholics who are anti-liberal. Only in this way can we hope for victory against liberalism, which is the most despicable and disastrous doctrine of all time.

Lord Our God: According to my great father St. Augustine, you know how to extract good from the evil that you permit. In your goodness, make the war that afflicts us serve to demarcate the camps, scatter the dreadful confusion that many have fomented in the Catholic camp to the advantage of the enemy, and establish and strengthen unity among good Catholics.

So that this unity is firm and enduring, it is necessary that it be founded on charity, the true love of God that consists, according to our Divine Master Jesus Christ, in keeping his commandments. Only as practicing Catholics can we be united with sincerity and constancy to face the sacrifices, bear the work, and overcome the difficulties that are demanded by the great cause that we must defend.

To be Catholics in this manner, which is the only way to be Catholics, let us begin with the observance of Holy Lent. We can carefully use the abundant resources for sanctification that the Church grants us in this time more than in any other.

Let us recognize in the things that afflict us the hand of God who punishes us for our sins and for not giving him the glory that we could give for the many years that he gave us to do so without the enemy being able to impede this. When punishment does not lead to penance, the situation gets worse. Let us ask pardon from God, then, humble and contrite, and weep over our sins and our great evils, so that it is not said of us what Salvio said when the enemies of Rome advanced closer and the city inhabitants thought only of amusement: "The people die, but laugh."

Let us weep over our sins, then, and go up to Calvary with Jesus Christ, but with the Cross, to die on it, if it is necessary, as that is how the heroes of Catholicism, the martyrs, die. Let us weep over our sins and be ready to drink the chalice of suffering before we are degraded by vice and the shameful mark of cowards and traitors to the faith and the country. Let us weep for our sins, but at the same time, let us march ahead in our campaigns for the triumph of morality, justice, and religion!

Most holy Heart of Jesus! In spite of the offense that we have committed against you by not desiring to consecrate this republic, always conserve the loving desire to set your divine fire on earth so that it burns. Divine Heart, set an abundance of this fire in this disgraced nation that suffers so much, so that the heart of all its sons burn with the desire to serve you and give you glory, and, finally, officially and solemnly consecrate it to you without reference to humans and childish fears that offend and hurt you. Let these bitter days of testing already end. Take away the punishment and look upon us with mercy in response to the requests of so many souls in this nation that adore and love you, in response to the blood of so many sons of the faith that has been shed for your glory, and in response to this cry that comes forth from the Catholic camps and declares, "Glory to God. Let us go forward with religion and the fatherland!" If this is not enough, Sacred Heart, take into account your agonies, sufferings, and infinite merits.

Your bishop asks this and desires that you all fervently request it from the Sacred Heart of Jesus. Your bishop blesses you in the name of the Father ✠ and of the Son ✠ and of the Holy Spirit ✠. Amen.

This letter will be read in all the churches of our diocese on the first Sunday immediately after its reception.

Given and undersigned for us, sealed with our seal, and countersigned by our secretary, in Pasto, on the day of St. Vincent the Martyr, January 22, 1902.
✠ Fr. Ezequiel, *Bishop of Pasto.*
Sent by the Reverend Anselmo Guerrero, Secretary.

CIRCULAR
LETTERS

Either with Jesus Christ or Against Jesus Christ

EITHER CATHOLICISM OR LIBERALISM

To the beloved members of my diocese

M Y CHILDREN, I DEDICATE THESE short pages to you. I wrote them especially for you. The goal is to erase from your understanding and hearts the bad impression that might have been caused by the letter of the priest D. Baltasar Vélez to Dr. D. Carlos Martínez Silva. This letter, in the form of a pamphlet entitled *Los Intransigentes*, spread widely in all the towns and, I think, throughout the Republic.

I did not make this small writing in the form of a pastoral letter because such a form is not appropriate for this. Its purpose is to dispel the errors that the priest expressed in the letter. Nevertheless, I would not like to give the impression that this matter is of less importance than if it had been released in the form of a pastoral letter. May God grant the healthy results that I look for and desire.

—✠ Fr. Ezequiel, *Bishop of Pasto.*

INTRODUCTION

The main point of the letter of the priest D. Baltasar Vélez is *a false spirit of conciliation with everything*. He connects with the way of thinking that certain liberal-Catholic men have established. The propagation of this idea would bring the worst consequences for religion and society.

In his letter, the aforementioned priest desires and pleads for *compromise* with liberalism in Colombia. He requests this from the clergy above all. We want to assume his good intentions, but he has certainly caused a scandal with good people with his letter. He has also provided no little pleasure for the enemies of the Church, judging from the conduct of those in this city of Pasto. Within very few days, many copies of the letter were made at the print shop of Ramírez and Gómez Hermanos in this very city. They are always in the devil's service. We have seen from there many sorts of works that we have had to prohibit.

The horror caused in good people by the priest's letter, and the obvious pleasure that it produced in the Church's enemies, should be enough for every good Catholic to judge it as contrary to the doctrines and interests of our holy religion, and to pray to God that He enlighten the unfortunate author. I would have left it at that, and prayed to God to give his light to the author of the letter, but certain clergy and laity expressed their very strong wishes that I say something against the letter. They gave me as a reason the fact that some of the faithful were vacillating in the truth because the author is a priest. This prompted me to say something. I will limit what I have to say. Time does not allow me to say the many things that could be said against the range of ideas that were set out in a capricious, vague, confused, rash, and suspicious manner.

This letter is in effect a genuine arrangement of good and bad, truth and error, obscure and rash doctrine, affirmations that, depending on how you see them, seem to be negations and negations that could be seen as affirmations, according to the side that is taken. In such confusion, it is almost impossible to establish a perfect demarcation of everything. It would be no small task to go through the entire letter line by line and point out different parts as erroneous, reckless, suspect, and contradictory. Above all, many parts would require my explanations to address these issues of contradiction, deceit, recklessness, error, and even heresy.

The near impossibility of saying everything that could be said against the letter leads me to propose to select from this muddle the capital errors or sources of errors. I will point them out in each of the chapters in which I refute them. God's greater glory and the good of souls are the sole things that move me to enter into this new combat that has arisen and to engage in a battle that, in this world, we can expect to bring forth only an abundance of insults, mockery, scorn, and horrible slander. I have already received these things for a long time from the enemies of God and his holy Church.

I

A great error found in the letter that
is contrary to the Catholic truth.

Before entering into combat against other errors, we believe it is appropriate to draw attention to a truly notable item in the introduction to the letter of Father D. Baltasar Vélez. As soon as the above-mentioned reverend negates a Catholic truth or displays ignorance of this truth, which is treated by all theologians, he undoubtedly falls into discredit for every sensible person, as does, consequently, his letter.

The reverend father states that on his ordination day, he promised that "he saw neither conservatives, nor liberals, nor Catholics, nor heretics in men, but *unity in Christ*."

To see in all men *unity in Christ*, even when some or many of these men admit and spread heresies, is not to see with the clear light of faith, but with the dark flame of error. Our Holy Mother Church has never and will never see in these men *unity in Christ*, but, on the contrary, has and will see in them separated members of the Church.

145

Canon 8 of the First Council of Nicaea points out the conditions for admitting heretics *who want to return to the Church*. Canon 6 of the First Council of Constantinople teaches that heretics are *uprooted, separated* from the Church.

The Church Fathers expressed themselves in the same way. St. Jerome's last point in the dialogue against the Luciferians is that "heretics are not Christ's Church, but the Antichrist's synagogue." My great father St. Augustine (in Serm. 1, c. 6 *De Simb. ad catechumen*) expresses it in these terms: "All the heretics left the Church like useless branches cut off from the vine." No other councils or Church Fathers need to be cited.

If, then, the heretics are separated from the Church, and Jesus Christ is the head of the Church, we can deduce in a clear and definite way that they are separated from Jesus Christ and are not *one with him*.

Jesus Christ himself, the Eternal Truth, teaches us that there are men who are separated from him, as we see in these words that come from his divine mouth: "As the branch cannot bear fruit of itself, unless it abide in the vine, so neither can you, unless you abide in me" (John 15:4).

Concerning believers who fall into mortal sin, one cannot say with certainty that they are *one with Jesus Christ*. Only charity unites us to Jesus Christ in a perfect way. Those who lose this unity through sin can only be united to him in an imperfect way through the gift of faith. In referring to this, St. John says, "He that committeth sin is of the devil" (1 John 3:8). He also says, "Whosoever is not just, is not of God" (1 John 3:10).

Even when we endeavor to give the kindest interpretation to the words of the author of the letter, there always remains an error that is contrary to the Catholic truth, that is, that heretics are *one in Christ* with believers.

The consequence of everything that has been stated

is the following dilemma: either the author of the letter wrote this error with the knowledge of what he was writing, or out of ignorance. If he did so with knowledge, he is lacking in faith because he teaches a doctrine that is contrary to the Catholic truth. Therefore, he and his letter are to be judged by all of the Church's faithful children. If he did so out of ignorance, we cannot hope that whoever is ignorant of such a clear Catholic truth can be a master who teaches and properly explains such difficult and delicate Catholic questions as are addressed in the letter. Nothing more needs to be added so that sensible people look at the letter with the scorn that it deserves. But I have promised to say something more, and will keep my promise.

II

Republicanism is not political liberalism,
as the author of the letter assures us.

True Catholics by now do not confuse nor cannot confuse liberalism with any form of government after the Pope, in his Encyclical *Immortale Dei*, taught the following: "Among the various forms of government, there are none that are reprehensible in themselves, since they do not contain anything that rejects Catholic doctrine; rather, through wise and just practice, they can maintain the state in perfect order." This perfectly agrees with these words from the Encyclical *Libertas*: "Again, it is not of itself wrong to prefer a democratic form of government, if only the Catholic doctrine be maintained as to the origin and exercise of power. Of the various forms of government, the Church does not reject any that are fitted to procure the welfare of the subject; she wishes only—and this nature itself requires—that they should be constituted without involving wrong to any one, and especially without violating the rights of the Church."

As we see, the Church accepts all forms of government, but does not confuse any of them with political liberalism. Political liberalism concerns more than form, and can be perfectly distinguished from it. Republicanism is a form, and nothing more than that. Political liberalism is something else, and is not a form because it can be united to all forms, and can also exist without any.

History offers us various examples of republics that were not darkened by political liberalism. It also offers us, even today, monarchies that are completely liberal in their politics. Republicans are the citizens of these American republics, and still there are many of these individuals who have nothing to do with political liberalism. On the contrary, there are many totally liberal monarchs in their politics in Russia, Germany, Italy, and elsewhere.

No, it is not true that republicanism is political liberalism. If this were so, here in Colombia, where everyone supports the republican form, and everyone is a republican, everyone would have to call themselves liberals. How come there are so many here who don't call themselves this? Despite everyone being republican, why are there still two sides, as in Europe, one calling itself liberal and the other not? Oh! It is because republicanism and political liberalism are very different things. Republicanism is a question of the pure form of government, and political liberalism is a question of doctrines. With this great difference between these two things, the obvious conclusion is that republicanism is not political liberalism, despite the assurances of the letter's author.

III

The political liberalism that is defended by the author of the letter is also condemned by the Church.

I sincerely confess that I read the letter of Father D. Baltasar several times in order to come to understand what it is that he understands by political liberalism, or what type of political liberalism he defends as good and innocent. The various definitions that he gives for this liberalism are the causes of ambiguity and confusion which made it difficult for me to grasp the nature of the object that he defines and proposes. In the end, I came to sufficient clarity to be able to judge that the political liberalism that he proposes and defends in the letter, even in this form, is condemned by the Church.

We have already seen that political liberalism is not republicanism, contrary to what the author of this letter states. What other things does political liberalism include, according to this author? What other definition does he give us? He writes the following: political liberalism "is the teaching of the doctrine that recognizes innate rights in man, and the right of nations to govern themselves freely and in an orderly manner."

This is a vague, indeterminate, broad-based definition. It can be accepted without problem by a rationalist or an atheist, but not without suspicion by a Catholic when he sees that the letter discusses the *rights of man, and the free government of the peoples*. These phrases ring very badly in the ears of every true believer for a long time. It certainly wouldn't be wrong for a Catholic to be suspicious of such a definition because later the author explains this in the letter. He expresses not a little pleasure because *humanity emancipated itself* with the memorable success of August 4, 1789.[1] He closes with another definition in which he states that political liberalism is the "Declaration of the rights of man." There it is!

Catholic Church teaching, which is defended by Catholic writers, asserts that the "Declaration of the rights of man" stems from rationalism, that this declaration

---

1 Day on which the privileges of the nobility and clergy were abolished along with feudalism by the National Assembly.

proposed these rights in theory, and that the Revolution implemented these in practice by applying them to politics and to the governing of the nation. In his encyclical *Immortale Dei*, Leo XIII states the following: "But that harmful and deplorable passion for innovation which was aroused in the sixteenth century first of all threw into confusion the Christian religion, and next, by natural sequence, invaded the precincts of philosophy, whence it spread amongst all classes of society. *From this source, as from a fountain-head, burst forth all those later tenets of unbridled license which, in the midst of the terrible upheavals of the last century,* were wildly conceived and boldly proclaimed as the principles and foundation of that new conception of law which was not merely previously unknown, but was at variance on many points with not only the Christian, but even the natural law."[2]

In consideration of this document, I do not think it necessary to remind readers that the "Declaration of the rights of man" was condemned by Pius VI when it appeared in France during the Revolution. We must also consider that the *Syllabus* condemns the errors of modern liberalism. The Declaration contains all of these errors in rudimentary form.

The principles that were fabricated by the Revolution of the past century, which are the foundation of the new rights, were thus condemned. The Church has only ever, and will only ever, condemn the principles of '89 for modern ideas; in other words, the new rights that are based on these dreadful human rights.

Now that it has been sufficiently proven that political liberalism, of which the author of this letter writes, is condemned by the Church, nothing more needs to be added. However, we will present further evidence.

---

2   Moreno's italics.

The author of the letter claims that the political liberalism that he defends is the one advocated by countless
nations that he goes on to name. One of those is, as he
calls it, *the Great North American Republic*. Well, in the
encyclical that he directed to the bishops of this republic,
Leo XIII confesses that the Church, under the protection
of absolute arbitrariness, is able to exist and operate there.
He then adds these words: "Whatever the truth of these
observations, it is no less necessary to reject *the error
that consists in believing that it is necessary to look in
America for the ideal of the Church, or that it would be
entirely legitimate and advantageous that the interests of
civil society and those of religious society walk separately,
as in the American custom.*"

If, then, the political liberalism that the author of the
letter espouses is the same as the one professed by the
North American Republic, we must conclude that this
is not the ideal of the Church. Nor is it legitimate or
advantageous for religion and society.

IV

*A further discussion of political liberalism
and its condemnation by the Church.*

In the previous chapter, I specified the political liberalism
that we need to fight against and that the author of the
letter defends. I believe that it will be useful and advantageous to surpass these limits in order to say something
more. In this chapter, therefore, I will explicate the doctrine of the Church concerning this liberalism to make
its wickedness better known and to judge and condemn
it just as it judges and condemns the Church.

Liberalism's cherished ideal is to undermine all obedience of the state, family, and individual to God and to his
holy Church so its advocates can declare themselves completely independent. To bring about this ideal, liberalism

does not stop at arguments, theories, and abstractions, but turns to the terrain of actions. In this terrain, it has shown, and shows, that it is essentially a political-religious system, and that the deep-thinker Donoso Cortés is correct in stating, "All political questions come back to the question of metaphysics and religion."

Political liberalism is rationalism in practice. This is what our Holy Father Leo XIII teaches in his encyclical *Libertas* with the following words: "What *naturalists* or *rationalists* aim at in philosophy, the supporters of *liberalism*, carrying out the principles laid down by naturalism, are attempting in the domain of morality and politics."

As I already stated, the *Rights of man* proposed a pseudo-philosophy, and the Revolution put this into practice. I say the same thing about the contemporary situation. I am supported by Leo XIII's words that rationalism teaches errors, and liberalism puts these into practice in politics or the government of the nations.

Liberalism's application of the principles of rationalism to politics can be small- or large-scale because, according to Leo XIII, "the will can separate itself from the obedience that is due to God and to those who participate in his authority in various ways and degrees, and for whom liberalism takes on many forms."

In his encyclical *Libertas*, Leo XIII points out three principal forms. The first is that which absolutely rejects God's supreme dominion over man and society. For this, it calls itself *radial* liberalism. The second is that which declares that mandates, which are derived from natural reason, need to be obeyed, but not those that God wants to establish in another way, that is, through the supernatural means of his Church. This is called *naturalist* liberalism. Leo XIII describes the third form or class of liberalism with these words: "Somewhat more moderate, but no less consequential for themselves are liberals who say that, in effect, life and habits of individuals are to be regulated according to the divine laws, but not the life of the state, because we are permitted to abandon the precepts of God for public issues. These precepts do not need to be considered when passing laws. The harmful resulting thought that *it is necessary to separate the Church from the state* comes from this. It is easy to see the absurdity in this, when the citizen respects the Church, and the state does not."

We have copied letter by letter what our Holy Father teaches about this form of liberalism, with the full intention of noting that this is what was proclaimed in Bogotá on August 20 by the delegates of the convention of the Liberal Party in their manifesto. In this manifesto, signed September 15, the delegates clearly and definitively state that, "though differing from the religious feelings of the great majority of the country and *though believing that the scientific solution to the so-called religious problem is* THE SEPARATION OF CHURCH AND STATE, the convention admits that the two powers need to be regulated according to a concordat."

What an insult to the majority of the country! The great majority already know this. Colombia's Catholics know it. The delegates of the convention of the Liberal Party believe that, if they come to power or head a government, they have to look at our holy religion as something foreign, as something that they do not have to pay attention to, despite it being the religion of the majority. Only for favors and out of consideration for the fact that it is the religion of the majority will they allow a concordat. But despite this concordat, "freedom of worship in its most generous application and the absolute liberty of the press will be established, without the most minimal limitations." These are the two liberties of doom that are noted in the manifesto. But all the other

153

modern liberties are presented as well, with their logical consequences. The Church and faithful of Colombia will suffer if the liberals come to govern!

In addition to these three forms of liberalism, there are a few less important principles and variations, according to how strong rationalist principles and their application to politics and government are. All of them, however, are condemned by the Church and should be abominated, because all of them share the same rationalist criteria that proclaims man's independence from God's authority, even if some aim for more independence than others.

V

The author of the letter does not mention that there is a Catholic liberalism, or a liberal Catholicism, that is condemned by the Church.

Though repugnant and seemingly odd, it must be assumed as true that a Catholic liberalism, or liberal Catholicism, exists. The contrary would require the acceptance of the absurdity and deception of ourselves and all those who say: *I am Catholic, but liberal.* Even worse would be the necessity to accept the still graver absurdity that Popes Pius IX and Leo XIII lied to themselves and us in referring so frequently to Catholic liberals and in condemning their conduct. Catholics cannot accept that the vicars of Christ mislead themselves and us in these matters. On the other hand, we know not a few men who shout and say in every way that they are liberals but also Catholics. Therefore, we have to agree that there exists a liberal Catholicism, even though Catholicism and liberalism are opposite things and there can be no union of the two.

I'm not going to say what liberal Catholicism is, or its seductiveness and damage to the holy Church and souls. In his many briefs and public addresses with which he has condemned this error, Pius IX has said all of this much better than I can. It is enough that we copy a few principal parts of these documents in order to know what it is, so that we can stick to the matter at hand. Many good citations are available, but we will use only a few.

In 1871, he stated to a French group of pilgrims, "What afflicts your country and blocks it from meriting God's blessings is the confusion of principles. I'll spell it out, and will not keep silent. What I fear for you are not these unfortunates of the *Commune*, who are true demons who have escaped from hell. It is Catholic liberalism, which is to say, this fatal system that always dreams of reconciling two irreconcilable things, the Church and revolution. I have already condemned this, and will condemn it forty times if necessary. Yes, I'll say it again on account of my love for you. Yes, this merry-go-round is what will destroy religion among you in France."

In a brief from May 8, 1873, directed to Belgian Catholic circles, he said the following: "What we most praise in your religious undertaking is your absolute aversion that you reportedly profess against Catholic-liberal principles and your strenuous intent to uproot them. Truly, when you devote yourselves to the fight against this insidious error, an error that is more dangerous than an openly-declared enemy because it covers itself in a cloak of zeal and charity and through this effort attempts to separate the simple people, you are getting rid of an unfortunate root of discord, and are making a significant contribution to uniting and strengthening souls."

In another brief on June 9 of the same year to the Catholic Society of Orleans, he said, "Even when you have to fight against ungodliness, the danger from this side is perhaps lighter than the threats from friends who are imbued with this amphibian doctrine that rejects the ultimate consequences of the errors and obstinately retains its seeds."

I bring to an end these citations with the brief from July 28, 1873 to the bishop of Quimper in which, making reference to the General Assembly of Catholic Associations, he expresses himself in this way: "You can place them on the slippery path of error, these so-called liberal opinions, which are accepted by many Catholics who, in other ways, are good and pious men. The very influence that their religion and piety has over them can very easily attract their spirits and lead them to profess very harmful beliefs. Instill, therefore, honorable brothers, in the members of this Catholic assembly, the belief that we inveigh so many times against the minions of these liberal opinions. I do not have in mind the Church's declared enemies, because it would be pointless to denounce them. I refer to those previously mentioned. They retained the hidden virus of liberal principles that they were nourished on with their milk, as if they were not impregnated with palpable evil, but with something as harmless for religion as they thought. It therefore easily contaminated their spirits and spread the seed of these disturbances that for so long brought revolution to the world."

These briefs closed all avenues to liberal-Catholics, or amphibians, as it was very well said in one of them. Not even the label "liberal" is clear of censure. Leo XIII in his Address to the Consistory of Cardinals on June 30, 1889 stated the following: "We cannot understand how people can say that they are Catholic and at the same time not only have sympathy for liberalism, but are blind and foolish to the extent that they glory in *calling themselves liberals*."

Liberalism is condemned by our holy mother Church in all its forms and degrees. All who see themselves as good Catholics must also condemn it in the same way, and go so far as to reject the *name "liberal."*

VI

*It will be proven that there are not a few liberals
in Colombia, as the author of the letter claims, who
profess liberalism as condemned by the Church.*

To prove what I propose in the present chapter, it is not
necessary to discourse at length nor seek reasons. The
author of the letter does all of that. He provides this
in abundance in his written arguments against what he
himself says, that is, against the affirmation that there
are *a few* liberals who here in Colombia profess the liberalism that is condemned by the Church.

First of all, the author of the letter confesses in a
conclusive way that he has many liberal friends. It is
natural to assume that these many liberal friends of the
author of the letter profess, at least, the political liberalism that he refers to and discusses. Yet seeing that this
liberalism has already been condemned by the Church,
we can conclude that there are many who advocate for
the liberalism that is condemned by the Church.

The author states elsewhere in the letter, "There are
many conservatives in Colombia who are deists and
materialists; *many* who believe very little about religious
matters, and *many* who are indifferent free thinkers." Do
these individuals not advocate the liberalism that is condemned by the Church, even though they give themselves
different names? There are, then, *many*, and not *a few*.

The author of the letter also reports that liberals here
in Colombia "insult the clergy in newspapers, mock religion's dogmas, establish freemasonry, declare Bentham's
teaching as official, usurp the patronage right,[3] the tithe,
and other goods of the Church, suppress convents, most

---

3   The Republic of New Granada, the state that preceded Colombia, inherited the Church's right of patronage from the Spanish
crown after its independence. In 1853, the liberals' separation
of Church and State abolished this. [German translator's note.]

criminally exile the holy Archbishop Mosquera,[4] expel the Jesuits once and then again in 1861, kick out bishops, wipe out religious communities, chase monks out of their monasteries with pistol whips, steal thirty or more million pesos worth of goods from the Church, strip from the clergy the right to hold elections and be elected themselves, re-establish Bentham's teaching as official and eliminate religious teaching in schools, once again exile the bishops and persecute priests, steal from cemeteries, establish the hateful law of civil marriage in practice, convert churches into barracks and priests into soldiers, shoot and hack at sacred images," etc.

When the author of the letter wrote this long and horrifying criminal report, was he still convinced that there are only *a few* liberals in Colombia who profess the liberalism that is condemned by the Church? We don't believe it. Only a few would not be able to commit these abuses and crimes in the presence of so many true Catholics who would undoubtedly have blocked them if they tried to do these things.

To counter the force of the preceding argument, it cannot be argued that what he said refers to the past, and that the liberals of today are not the same. That may have been believed before the convention of the Liberal Party in Bogotá that welcomed delegates from all *departamentos*.[5] But after the delegates, as representatives of the Liberal Party, declared what they must do if they form the government, the policies they must establish, that are contrary to Catholic doctrine and morals, and

4 Manuel José Mosquera (1800–1853) was archbishop of Bogota from 1835 until 1852. He was exiled in that year for opposing recent laws that placed the Church under state power. He went to New York City, where his brother lived, and thence to Europe, where he died.

5 Colombia was and is divided into administrative districts called *departamentos*.

the scorn with which they must look on the Church and our holy religion, there is no doubt that liberals of today are the same and think the same as liberals of the past.

To all those who we have indicated to be liberals who profess the liberalism that is condemned by the Church, we must add individuals whom we hear frequently saying, "I am Catholic and believe everything that our holy mother Church believes, but I am a liberal in politics." We include everyone who says this. As we have already seen, and it is proved, liberal Catholicism and liberal Catholics are condemned. It must be concluded that, contrary to what the author of the letter says, there are not a few in Colombia who profess the liberalism that is condemned by the Church.

VII

There are many practical liberals in Colombia, and it is fitting to speak of them and of others for their own good.

If we adhere to the rigors of the laws of argumentation, there is no doubt that we can call all partisans of liberalism practical liberals once we have established that liberalism is an eminently practical system and that it does not stop at speculations and theories. What is the purpose of this chapter, then, that is dedicated to proving that practical liberals exist in Colombia, when we have already proven the existence of liberals? This chapter seems unnecessary, but in reading it, we can see that it is anything but unnecessary.

The liberals who are examined here differ from the others in their works, but not their ideas. We can say, then, that practical liberals are those who do not admit any error of liberalism, but who still act in civil and political life as if they were such liberals. I refer to these, and I say it is fitting to discuss them, for their own good and for the good of others. It would be a favor for them when, seeing what is pointed out here, they recognize themselves, repent, and return to God. This would be a favor for others too if by reading this they avoid falling into practical liberalism.

It is nearly impossible to list all those who express themselves, in one way or another, as practical liberals because there are an incalculable number of varieties of forms. I can only point out those who appear most significant to me. In this chapter, this will concern only one class, which is the following.

"Those who are under the direction of liberal leaders and are always ready to carry out their orders." These, as can be clearly seen, are affiliated with the party, and even call themselves liberals. They still say, on the other hand, that they condemn each and every one of liberalism's liberties of perdition, that they attend the Mass, perhaps pray the rosary, and *go so far as to pay the first fruits and go to confession.* The author of the letter states these as reasons to exempt them from complicity in liberalism and its heinous crimes. But are they exempt from responsibility and guilt before God? No, they are, rather, the great accomplices to all the sins, abuses, and evil of this party in which they accepted a position, in which they are publicly listed, and for which they are willing to support, defend, exalt, and elevate, if they can, to the height of power.

It needs to be said without any doubt that to this group belong these thousands of unfortunate farmers affiliated with the liberal party. In the morning, these farmers go to Mass and receive the priest's or sometimes the bishop' blessings, and in the evening go and declare to their liberal leader that they are ready for the moment when they are called upon, to vote for the liberal candidate, or to go to war. They note that they will pay no heed to what the priests say, or that they will shackle them when the time comes.

These men sign themselves up, put themselves at the service of their leaders, and wait for the orders to follow in every way possible, however criminal they are. Do we have to state once again the great stupidity that argues that it is contrary to the principles of Christian morals that these men be exempt from responsibility and guilt before God? Have we not already seen that these masses have profaned churches, destroyed images, tied up bishops and priests, and not respected anything, however holy it is, when their leaders ordered them to commit these crimes? Will we still say that they do not have any responsibility or guilt?

Even supposing that these men do not know all the details of liberalism's wickedness, they are still not exempt from responsibility. Even those most profoundly ignorant have to escape this ignorance of so much damage caused to religion and society because the question emerges of who is responsible for the revolution? Is it perhaps the eight or twelve people from every village who give speeches and write liberal articles? We have to admit that these people do promote revolution, but could they carry this out without the participation and assistance of these men of the people? No, they could not execute this to the end. Liberalism, as a consequence, would remain in their heads, unapplied to the government of the people.

Even when, then, certain individuals among the people are in complete ignorance of liberalism's wickedness (which I do not concede), it is of utmost urgency to give them instruction and lift them out of this ignorance, because the good of both religion and the people depends on them. I do not agree with certain voices (some very respectable) who say that the people are entirely Catholic, and we should leave them in peace and say nothing. Some voices said the same thing in Ecuador before the last revolution when a servant of God, driven by his zeal and seeing things as they are, warned the people about cursed liberalism. There is no need to preach on this. Here, the people are all Catholic; everyone has faith, and everyone professes the doctrines of our holy mother Church.

The disillusionment—the bitter disillusionment—that then came to these people means that they now lament their naiveté. I think there would have been nothing to fear in a country like this if the people had been made to understand their responsibility and guilt before God for affiliating with the liberal party and to understand the poor situation of their souls that resulted from their willingness to obediently follow liberal leaders in whatever was ordered. If, after explaining all of this, they continue in their evil attitude, the principles of moral theology teach us how their priest and confessor should act towards them. I say this because I believe that the glory of God and the salvation of souls depend on this.

VIII

There are other practical liberals.

In the preceding chapter I made known the practical liberals who are complicit in the sins and crimes of liberalism. Now I will point out others who, even if they are not numbered among the major and primary accomplices, like those already mentioned, are still not exempt from complicity with liberalism, and therefore from guilt and responsibility before God.

It is certain and indisputable that the liberal party of Colombia is anti-Catholic, as noted in the manifesto of the convention of the party that took place in Bogotá, and that is dated last September 15 [1897]. It is clear that all those who cooperate in some way in contributing to, promoting, and giving life to this party are complicit with liberalism and responsible before God.

Once again I warn you that I am only going to point out those who appear to me to be the most complicit because it is not possible to speak of everyone in this little writing. The complicit are the following:

1. Those who give their vote to liberal candidates. They cooperate so that these candidates are voted to councils, the assembly, the congress, the vice presidency, or the presidency. These are people who speak, propose, vote, and mandate policies due to their doctrinal errors. Therefore, those who place these people in a position of power to damage religion and scandalize their neighbors are responsible before God.

2. Those who contribute financially to improving the organization of the liberal party. They are practical liberals and accomplices to liberalism. This includes those who did much in recent months by making contributions so that delegates could go to the convention. They have done the same on other occasions to help spread liberal writings, hold liberal gatherings, or carry out projects that give the party energy, force, and life.

3. Those who attend liberal gatherings, participate in the funerals of liberals, are members of liberal organizations, those who cheer on men in their liberal works, and those who praise and applaud those who give liberal addresses. They are practical liberals and are responsible before God.

4. Those who subscribe to liberal periodicals are practical liberals because their financial support of the periodical contributes to the propagation of liberalism. They provide a poor example to those

who see this and cause them to do likewise. They also give their family members the opportunity to read material that is inappropriate due to the danger it poses of losing or weakening faith. The same can be said of those who print, share, sell, or announce such periodicals, brochures, or evil books.

5. Those who send their children or dependents to liberal schools or colleges. They are practical liberals. Providing the occasion for spiritual ruin, they are therefore responsible for this ruin. They are also contributing to the support of the school and giving it greater importance, and must also be held responsible for this.

6. Those who praise certain liberal colleges, schools, and publications are complicit in liberalism. In this respect, self-declared Catholic journalists frequently fail. They sometimes go to the extreme. They sometimes go so far as to work up the fathers of families to send their children to liberal centers of teaching. They weigh the qualities of the *enlightened and competent male director* and the great pledges of the *virtuous and pleasant female director.* Others stoke curiosity and guide some towards liberal writings, praising the literary merit of the work, the diversity, and the acceptability of the reading to the heavens, without bearing in mind that the more attractive something is, the more dangerous it is.

This conduct of these writers who extol their Catholic selves is inexplicable. Likewise, it is inexplicable how, after writing an article enthusiastically in favor of the Catholic religion, a writer then turns to the works of Voltaire, Diderot, Renan, and others. It is also inexplicable how they say that they wish that certain journals (such as the demonic Mephistopheles) had many subscribers and a long life, and are unhappy when they stop publishing.

It is strange to see these things in Colombian journals that fight in the camp that opposes liberalism. We highlight this so that those with eyes can see and attempt to mend their ways. A good Catholic must regret it when a liberal college opens or a liberal journal, brochure, or book appears, and rejoice with all of his soul when he sees these cease to exist.

7. Those who criticize the pope's encyclical, the bishop's pastoral letter, and the priest's sermon solely because the encyclical, pastoral letter, or sermon states something against liberalism. They are practical liberals and complicit in liberalism.

The question of complicity as taught by moral theology can be applied to all of these cases and to many others who are not pointed out here because it would become endless to do so.

IX

Another necessary and potentially very beneficial chapter concerning complicity with liberalism.

Because the author of the letter so ardently defends women who call themselves liberals, designates them angels of peace who pour out love and tenderness, greatly sympathizes with them, and regrets that they are reprimanded, I thought it necessary and useful to write this chapter solely on women who are practical liberals or accomplices of liberalism. I believe it to be necessary and useful. Here is this chapter, even if a certain class of people will not receive it well.

Our Lord Jesus Christ ordered the Gospel to be preached to all the peoples and that they be taught to observe all the things that were ordered. As this does not exclude anyone, women, the same as men, must also believe all the truths and observe all that has been mandated, because they will be held liable before God if they do the contrary.

Seeing that the Catholic truth and Christian morals are so uncompromising for men as for women, the following are also complicit in liberalism:

1. When they do one of the things already noted in the previous chapter, such as giving money for the purpose of the liberal party, attending liberal gatherings, praising liberal works and addresses, subscribing to liberal journals, and sending children or dependents to liberal colleges or schools.

2. Those who provide public support for the liberal party are complicit in liberalism. This complicity is greater the higher the social position of the woman who calls herself liberal, that is, her position based on talent, wealth, or other motives, because it is clear that this influence is positive for the party. Merely demonstrating affection or friendly relations with members of the liberal party does much for the party.

3. Women who wear red ribbons, deck out their houses and balconies with red cloth on holidays (this is done on religious festivals), with the exclusive objective of suggesting with these ribbons and red cloths that they support the liberal party, and want to see it win are complicit in liberalism.

4. Women who adorn the facades of their houses in order to receive liberal soldiers, who make and throw wreaths, and who cheer them with

enthusiasm and pleasure are also complicit.

5. Women who, when a revolution spreads or is already underway, embroider banners carried by liberal battalions and sew outfits for the soldiers, and even more so those who transport letters or important orders so that they reach their destinations more securely, and serve as spies in order to contribute to the greater success of liberals in publicized cases for the good of the party are equally complicit.

6. Women who display piety and devotion, who frequently go to confession and receive communion, but who publicly follow self-declared liberals, and commit the acts that we have already pointed out incur greater complicity with liberals. These women cause great damage to simple souls because, with their frequent reception of the sacraments and apparent devotion and piety, they deceive these souls. These latter thus think, "Don't people say that liberalism is bad? How is it that Mrs. Fulana calls herself liberal, spends time with other liberals, attends their gatherings, helps them, and declares publicly her desire that they win, *given how pious she is?*" These women do so much damage to souls and to the Church!

We will not point out the other many methods that make not a few women complicit with liberalism. No one is unfamiliar with these named individuals. Everyone knows that many women who call themselves liberals put this into practice here in Colombia. Also, the teachings of moral theologians about the sins of complicity can be applied to them.

If the author of the letter finds himself in the presence of God, and calmly and impartially thinks and meditates, he will not fail to agree that many women are indeed accomplices to liberals according to one or another of the indicated methods. In this case, I pray to Our Lord Jesus Christ that we do not go back to calling these women angels of peace, nor say that they are virtuous, nor praise their piety, because this is deception. They do more damage than if they damaged or burned down the houses they live in. Mercy vociferously demands that we tell them that they are committing evil and are sinners, so that they repent, stop their sins of complicity, and beg God for forgiveness and the grace that they sin no more.

X

Either for Jesus Christ, or against Jesus Christ.
The liberals who wage open war against Jesus Christ, and noisily and scandalously say whatever they want against everything connected to him; those who persecute him in a more moderate way without a great uproar; those who seek a way for liberalism, without ceasing to be such, to move hand in hand with Catholicism while harming this latter; and those who help and protect all those in their liberal scheming, are clearly and blatantly against Jesus Christ, and do not fight for the side that is with him. But there are some Catholics who believe that they can remain neutral, and not choose between the opposing sides that today compete to govern the people. The one side aspires to govern them according to the law of God and the teachings of the Church, and the other does not take into account anything that is mandated by God and taught by the Church. This is the other error that is necessary to drive away. The present chapter is dedicated to this.

This neutral state, this middle place which some Catholics want to occupy, is an illusion, a chimera, a complete deception. It has not existed and never will. This is what Jesus Christ declared in his gospel when he said, "Whoever is not with me is against me."

Some wanted to oppose this sentence to another which we read in St. Luke: "He that is not against you, is for you." Cornelius a Lápide and all the other expositors say that there is no opposition between these two sentences because the second one needs to be understood in the following way: He who is against you *in nothing*, is for you. This does not apply when one takes a neutral stance in religion, and for this the result is always that he who is not with Jesus Christ is against him.

Jesus Christ has full authority over nations, peoples, and individuals, and can impose his law with the full right to being obeyed. Nations, peoples, and individuals that are neutral and therefore indifferent to whether Jesus Christ is obeyed or not, are against him because they do not seek the proper obedience, and cease honoring him as they must as the sovereign Lord of all. They go so far as to allow him to be insulted and scorned.

Jesus Christ has the right to everything for himself and his glory. As a consequence, all must be ordered to this end in the governing of nations, peoples, families, and individual conduct. Those who do not seek this state of things, those who are indifferent to whether or not Jesus is given glory, to whether or not he is recognized as the sovereign Lord of all, or to whether or not he is being served, is against Jesus Christ.

From this we can conclude that a government, even one that does not issue laws of persecution against the Church of Jesus Christ, but with only the fact of its indifference to such laws, is already against Jesus Christ. An example will make this more easily understood. Let us suppose that a man suddenly forces his way into a house, menaces the housewife with the weapon he is holding, and demands her money or he will stab her in the chest. The woman's strong and robust son is in the house. He can easily defend his mother and free her from the danger. But, far from doing this, he says to himself: "My mother should figure this out as best she can. If she is robbed, she is robbed. If she does not want to give the money and she is killed, then she is killed. I don't have anything to do with that. I want to remain neutral." Who would not say that this son worked against his mother by the mere fact of not helping her when he could have? This is certain because his mother ended up hurt because her son had not defended her.

A government does the same when it observes the damage that is done to the religion of Jesus Christ, and says like this son: "Religion has to deal with this on its own. If God is blasphemed, then God is blasphemed. If errors that are contrary to doctrine are spread, then they are spread. If hearts are pulled away due to seduction, then they are pulled away. If religion totally disappears from the people, then it disappears. If Jesus Christ is completely forgotten, it's all the same to me. I have nothing to do with it. I must remain neutral." Who can doubt, when we ask once more, whether this government is against Jesus Christ?

The same rule can be applied to those individuals who can and must do something for Jesus Christ and don't. There are many people today like this who very brazenly state, "I don't get involved in politics. They can fix things. It doesn't matter who is in power. It's all the same to me whether one or the other is in power." Who cannot see that these men are against Jesus Christ since they don't care when men who persecute the Church, its ministers, and its affairs come to power.

There are many others who explain things in this manner: "What's happening is very sensitive. We are in great danger. The enemies of God work feverishly. But what can we do! I don't want to get into an argument with anyone! There is no reason to get upset with anyone."

Some or many who talk like this can do much for Jesus Christ due to their social status, talents, or many resources. They fail to do so, and leave the enemies of Jesus Christ to continue to work as long as these enemies of Jesus are their friends and do not persecute them as they do the Divine Master. Will we say that these individuals are with Jesus Christ when they are friends of his enemies and do not oppose war plans against Jesus Christ even though they can?

Enough: These neutral individuals will be judged by Jesus Christ with this statement that he declares against them: "Who is not with me, is against me."

XI

Either Catholicism or liberalism.
Reconciliation is not possible.

When dealing with a question that our mother the Church has spoken on, the true Catholic must always think and speak with her. He must not lose sight of the teachings that have already been given by the teacher of the truth if he wants to walk on firm and secure land. His own judgment must disappear when the Church provides its own.

Has the Church made known its judgment on compromises and reconciliation between Catholicism and liberalism? Yes, the Church has addressed this, and has condemned this reconciliation as harmful to religion and to souls. To support this affirmation, we will cite only one proposition that is condemned in the *Syllabus* along with an address and a brief by Pius IX. We will leave out other documents that prove the same thing and that could be cited.

The last proposition condemned in the *Syllabus* says the following: "The Roman Bishop can and should reconcile himself and make concessions to progress, liberalism, and modern civilization." That this proposition is condemned as erroneous means that the opposite is true, that is, that the pontiff cannot and should not reconcile himself or make concessions with progress, liberalism, or modern civilization. Catholicism, then, which is headed by the pope, cannot be reconciled with liberalism because it is incompatible with the faith. This solemn condemnation is already sufficient proof for every Catholic. However, we will also cite an address and a brief, as mentioned.

On September 17, 1861, with reference to the decree related to the canonization of the twenty-three Franciscan martyrs of Japan, Pius IX said the following:

> In these times of confusion and disorder, it is not rare to see Christians, Catholics—also some clergymen—who always talk about the middle-way, reconciliation, and compromise. Well, I do not hesitate to declare that these men are in error. I don't see them as any less dangerous enemies of the Church...Just as reconciliation between God and Belial is not possible, so it is between the Church and those who think of its destruction. Undoubtedly, our power must be led by wisdom, but no less must it be that a lack of wisdom would lead us to an agreement with unbelievers.... No, we must be firm: No reconciliation. No forbidden and impossible compromise.

The brief that we promised to cite is from the same Pius IX, addressed to the president and members of the *Circulo de San Ambrosio* of Milan on March 6, 1873, in which he says the following:

Although the sons of the world are wiser than the sons of the light, their frauds and violence would be less harmful if many who called themselves Catholics did not hold out a friendly hand. We do not lack people who wish to conserve friendship with them by means of doctrines that are called liberal-Catholic. They endeavor to establish a close partnership between the light and the darkness, and community between justice and iniquity. These doctrines, based on the most pernicious principles, flatter the worldly power that encroaches on spiritual things, and drags spirits to submit to, or at least to tolerate, the most iniquitous laws, as if it is not written, *no one can serve two masters.* These are much more dangerous and fatal than declared enemies either because, going unnoticed and perhaps not knowing it themselves, they support the attempts of evil, or because they express honest and sane doctrine that trigger hallucinations in foolish lovers of reconciliation and deceive the honest who oppose open error.

The Church, then, spoke so energetically, expressively, and categorically of the prohibition of reconciliation between Catholics and liberals that there is not the smallest doubt. If, then, the Church has addressed and condemned this reconciliation, no one can propose or accept doing so, and those who propose or accept such reconciliation are working against what the Church teaches and desires.

It is necessary to teach this doctrine in such a loud tone so that all hear it, and hear it clearly, and that all understand it. Making the words of Pius IX my own, and applying them to our current situation, I conclude this chapter by saying that we find ourselves in times of confusion and disorder. In these days, Christians, Catholics (a priest too) launched to the four winds words of the middle course, compromise, and reconciliation. Well, I do not hesitate to declare that these men are in error. I also do not hold them to be the least dangerous of the enemies of the Church. Reconciliation between Jesus Christ and the devil, between the Church and its enemies, and between Catholicism and liberalism is not possible. No, let us be firm: either Catholicism or liberalism. Reconciliation is not possible.

XII

*It will be deduced from the preceding chapters
how unjust the invectives of the author of the
letter are against the clergy of Colombia.*

The letter's author hurls such bitter complaints, harsh recriminations, and injurious invective against Colombia's clergy for their preaching against liberalism and for revealing what liberals are that if he did not assure us that he was a priest, we would assume that he was a fervent anti-cleric.

The letter writer claims that Colombia's priests condemn liberalism without understanding what it consists of and with sermons that are supremely inappropriate. Not only this, but he also adds, with unspeakable boldness, that as soon as liberals give a little money to priests, these latter change color, no longer consider them to be bad, and forget their preaching against them. What slander and insults! Honorable priests! Join in with me in exclaiming, "Lord, pardon our brother and fill him with light and grace!"

If the author supported his claims, recriminations, and invective with a solid basis, the situation would be very sad in every way, and would not deserve the *transeat* of any claimants for the simple reason that the simple faithful have understood. But if these claims, recriminations, and invective are built on false foundations, the situation appears much sadder, and more distressing and lamentable.

On what does the author of the letter base his claims and invective against Colombia's clergy? We have already seen: he bases these on the false assumption that there are few liberals in Colombia. He asks, what explains these sermons against liberalism if there are no more political liberals here, that is, republicans, which we all are? Why these condemnations from the pulpit, if there are no more than a few here who profess the liberalism that is condemned by the Church? Above all, why all the attacks against women, given that they are all clerical, angels of peace, pious and good?

From all of the preceding chapters, we can deduce with clarity how unjust these recriminations are. Indeed, it has been proven that republicanism is not political liberalism; that political liberalism, even as explained by the author of the letter, is condemned by the Church; and, lastly, there are in Colombia many who profess the liberalism that is condemned by the Church and many accomplices. Since all of this has been proven, the entirely contradictory fundamentals of the author's claims, recriminations, and invective fall apart. The argument is therefore unfounded and unjust.

We will not deny, however, that there could be one or two priests who on some occasions spoke harshly regarding liberalism and liberals, or that they had worldly interests in mind when they spoke, whether his own or that of his family, or that they did not express the evil of this terrible error with all of the precision that such terms require. We will not deny that this could have occurred and, if it did, we do not seek to excuse imprudence, bad purposes, or ignorance. On the contrary, we regret these errors and wish that they had never been committed. But that is still no reason to no longer preach against liberalism. It is totally necessary to attack this error because it is the great danger for religion and for society. But the attack should not be badly done because this will aid the enemy. The attack must be prepared beforehand and, once prepared, given with serenity and strength of character, and always with the view of doing so for the good of souls and the glory of God.

I would have brought this chapter to an end with what was said, but the author of the letter is in error where he says that priests fall silent when they are given money. This needs to be refuted. After saying this, he adds, "In every case, their money (that of the liberals) is not to be avoided."

What does the author of the letter want for liberals? Does he want them exempt from certain obligations only because they are liberals? Does he want the Church to exempt them from paying tithes and first fruits, for the sole reason that they are rebel children? Are they not as obligated to follow these laws of the Church as obedient and compliant children are? The author knows very well, or should know, that they are obligated, even when they have had the misfortune of falling into heresy, because it is not just that they gain from their rebellion. Why is this observation made? It is said like it was a joke, but is in fact unfounded and unjust. If the priest witnesses the marriage of a liberal's son, conducts the funeral of the wife or daughter, or holds some other ministry function that they request, or at which he charges a fee, why should the liberal enjoy the privilege to which he has no right? The author of the letter should therefore see that *his grace* does not possess grace, reason, justice, or anything else good, but much bad.

The author's recriminations and invective are unjust, very unjust, to his brothers in the priesthood. All of them undoubtedly pardon him with their hearts and ask God to pardon him.

XIII

The author's erroneous concepts about the attitude of the Colombian clergy about the Conservative and Liberal Parties.

The author of the letter judges as a sin the support of the priests and opposition of the Liberal Party for the Conservative Party, which, he believes, converted the republic into a lake of blood. What things he says! What reasons he gives to condemn this attitude of the clergy!

We must confess that the author occasionally is not lacking in logic, and admirably extracts the consequences that emerge from the principles that he has set out. The shame is that the principles are false, and that the consequences are also false because this is the way of logic.

The writer of the letter repeatedly states that here in Colombia the bad liberalism of Europe does not exist, that there are only a few who profess the liberalism that is condemned by the Church, and that the conservatives and liberals are separated by political interests more than by religious ideas.

After these principles have been laid out, it is very logical for the author of the letter to admonish the Colombian clergy, to call them to examine their conduct, and to ask why they lean towards the conservative party and support it, and oppose the liberal party? Who cannot see the logic in these admonitions? If there are no differences in religious ideas between conservatives and liberals, if everyone is obedient and compliant with our Holy Mother Church, if some of them defend, protect, and love her, why do priests support the conservative party and oppose the liberal party?

Let us repeat that it is a pity that the principles stated by the author of the letter are false. If they were true, we would be able to joyfully extract the same beautiful consequences that he extracts. We would make no distinction between the two parties. We would advise everyone to see that they are united because they think the same thing. Union would not be difficult in this case, and would bring peace, well-being, abundance, and happiness. How much would we do and how much would we give if this were true! God knows only too well that we cannot refuse him so that all of this truth would be attained.

Today, unfortunately, what the author says in the letter is not true. Liberals have just stated publicly with their manifesto given in Bogotá that they are true liberals. There is no doubt, consequently, that they are enemies of the Church. The clergy have the duty not only to pray inside the parish church, but also to work outside, and to use everything licit at their disposal so that the Liberal Party does not come to govern the people with laws that make them independent of God and bring them to more complete destruction.

The author of the letter himself tells us what the Liberal Party of Colombia is for the Church and its ministers. It is not necessary to repeat the report of the horrendous crimes that this party committed because it is already available in another place. But it needs to be added that the author of the letter did not invent these crimes. He got them from history books that everyone can read, although truly this is unnecessary, because there are many living eyewitnesses who can testify, and there are still ruins of convents and haciendas of churches that were sold. Though silent, these are no less eloquent testimonies.

If the convention of the Liberal Party had not made its declarations, people would still be able to say that the liberals of today are not the same as those from before. But they have spoken, and there is no doubt that they are the same, which is to say, declared enemies of our mother the Church. How can the author of the letter, then, desire that we have the same considerations and give the same support to this party as to the Conservative Party? How come he has condemned the opposition of the clergy?

Priests must always fight as hard as possible in all things against whatever party is against Jesus Christ and his holy religion. The author of the letter believes that Colombia's clergy, his brothers in the priesthood, also approve of the element of the Conservative Party that is against Catholicism. No, the bad that is found in this party cannot be supported. This is condemned, just as everything that is evil in the Liberal Party is condemned.

The present fight is religious, even when the fight takes place on political terrain, because this is where liberalism is found. It is clear that priests have to take part in this fight, and support those most favorable to religion. Who can doubt that here in Colombia the party which is called Conservative has conducted itself much better in its relations with the Church than the Liberal Party? If the Church is better treated by the Conservative Party than by the Liberal, why is the author of the letter surprised that priests lean more to the Conservative Party and are opposed to the Liberals? Why does he condemn priests when they tell the faithful *in which ballot box and for whom* they need to deposit their votes when there are two candidates for election, one Catholic and the other liberal? In his encyclical *Sapientiae Christianae*, Leo XIII, in addressing this theme, declares, "Men of proven integrity who are worthy of being called Christian must be supported at the ballot box. There is no licit reason to support those who are against religion." Moral theologians have already told us this. Apparently, the author of the letter forgot at least some points of theology. That explains his erroneous ideas of the attitude of Colombia's clergy towards the Conservative and Liberal Parties.

XIV

*It is necessary to fight against liberalism
in a determined and unanimous way in
view of its alarming propagation among
us which has damaged our faith.*

We have already stated, demonstrated, and repeated that there are many liberals in Colombia. Many others are guilty of complicity with liberals. We can add that there are possibly even many more who are suspected of supporting liberalism without being aware of doing so.

Our holy faith has many enemies. These enemies do not sleep, rest, or stay idle, but continually move, work, and fight for their triumph. They govern with the smallest amount of Catholicism that is possible when they cannot totally banish it. They only permit it out of deference, as they say, for the religious sentiment of the great majority.

On account of this attitude, work, and constant and tenacious fight and movement of the enemy, their sphere of action is widened. The enemy bolsters its ranks, gains terrain, advances, and shows itself in public, where it not only requests, but also demands that its alleged rights to separate man from God, his Creator and Lord, be respected and that it legislate in a way that it can freely insult this great God and spread however many blasphemies that it can. As if it has a right to such crimes! If all rights come from God, there is no doubt that God cannot give any right to man to mock, insult, or work against him. Consequently, no one possesses these rights that are requested and asserted by liberalism. With what force would we like to stop the teaching of this doctrine! But this is not what we are discussing now, and so we must unfortunately leave it there.

We have stated that the enemy advances, bolsters his camp, and spreads. Yes, liberalism spreads everywhere.

It invades everything, like a deadly plague. I have seen many victims fall to its destructive action. I have seen the life of faith dying in some individuals, others who have suffered greatly from this terrible evil, and still others who, lacking firmness, are shaken and drunk from the asphyxiation produced by the contagious atmosphere that they breathe in. Many have already swallowed the venom without feeling it, and write, speak, and work like a liberal though they were previously in the camp of sane ideas.

Given that the enemy's attitude is so daring and worrying, and the danger to souls so great, it is necessary to fight with Christian valor if we do not want to be cowardly soldiers of the *militia Christi* who are unworthy of the name. It is not that every Catholic should grab his rifle or get others to do the same, because even the enemy does not use guns. If they did display guns, then it would be good for Catholics to do the same, and go out to meet them. If a nation can go to war for certain just causes, then it is much better to do so in order to defend their faith, since this provides ways not only to be happy on earth as much as possible, but also to reach the true and eternal happiness for which man was created. If we have no right to wage war in this case, we do not have it for any other because all of the other possible just motives fall far short of that of the preservation of the faith of a people. But I repeat that this is not about a bloody war, and I do not call for one. Let us never see one! I only say that, in view of the spread of liberalism and its arrogance. High and low social statuses, clergy and laity, young and old, rich and poor, and men and women all have the duty to legally defend our faith as much as each can, and to fight against liberalism, impede its propagation, and, if possible, end its doctrines and works.

The bishops of our ecclesiastical province of Colombia have already said many good things against the monster that threatens to swallow us. We recommend reading *La Semana Religiosa*, the organ of the diocese of Popayán, and *El Revisor Católico*, that of the diocese of Tunja, just to name two. In the last few months, very well-written articles combating liberal doctrines have appeared in many issues of these two. To the writer of the letter and to others who say with him that Colombia does not have the liberalism that the Church has condemned, I recommend in particular the most recent article that I have seen in *La Semana Religiosa* from the diocese of Popayán, entitled *Colombian liberalism*.

Supporting the views of the bishops, priests have held up very high the flag of integrity of the Catholic faith with their instructions to the people and brilliant writings. It is also necessary that the Catholic laity back up their bishops and priests, and loudly and clearly defend the faith. In view of a common enemy that provokes us to fight, nobody can remain inactive and idle.

Faith must be for the people the most valuable treasure. This treasure must be defended without the slightest diminishment so that it can be transmitted in its entirety to the next generation as the most precious legacy that we can leave. From this comes, then, the urgent duty for each Catholic to come to the defense of the faith when this is in danger, and to fight and oppose the enemy in whatever ways that God's law allows.

Today the enemy presents the religious battle in the political terrain. We must now come to this field with valor and decisiveness so that the leaders are Catholic, and their manner of governing the people, which is to say their politics, is Catholic. The Church has not and cannot make liberal candidates its own. Whoever gives such candidates their votes sins and offends God.

We can also oppose error, and use words to fight, that is, not remain silent when they speak against our holy religion in our presence. Those who can write can fight by opposing impious teaching or inadequate answers with fully Catholic doctrines. Everyone can do something against error with a good example, a good Catholic life, and prayer. We can ask God to enlighten the blind and bring wayward individuals back to the good path. We can also support good people in the faith and in the practice of the Christian virtues.

CONCLUSION

Many other chapters would be added to this little work that would be of no less interest than what we have already written. But we want this to be available quickly and obtained easily, and will therefore close with a few words.

The first thing is to assure from the heart that we hate no one and wish no one bad. We pray to God for abundant blessings for everyone and, above all, for eternal life, and that the goal of this writing is to contribute something to the triumph of the truth, the glory of God, and the good of souls.

After this declaration, we are ready for the flood of phrases of pure liberalism, which are already so old and smell of the warehouse where they are kept so it seems necessary to let in some fresh air. Obstinacy! Cover ups! Ministers of God should not get mixed up in politics! Their mission is a mission of peace! This is a lack of charity! Let all of this come. We have already heard more. But it needs to be said here that this small work only discusses religion, that although our mission is peaceful, it is also a war against all error, and that there is no lack of brotherly love in teaching the truth as the Church teaches. The charity that is so often preached by liberalism and its partisans is nothing but absurd and criminal tolerance that we will never have if we are in God's hands.

We hope that the author of the letter accepts with good will what we have said herein because, on the one hand, he says *that he humbly subjects his writing to the judgment of the Colombian episcopacy*; and on the other hand, he must assume that we have written against the errors of his letter, and not against him. We also hope that he accepts the following counsels that we offer:

1. That he does not boast of an independent character and also not say that he is never malleable for anyone, because this does not correspond with the perfection of Christian humility, and is a disposition of the spirit that is dangerously exposed to total spiritual ruin. Minimally, he must be tender, indulgent, easily-influenced, and easily molded by God, his holy religion, and his legitimate superiors.

2. That he does not leave so fast for North America and Europe, because there is a great lack of priests here in Colombia. The bishops need him for places that have no priests.

3. That he does not call Our Lord Jesus Christ *The People's Tribune*, nor add that he came to establish the rights of the people. All of this sounds revolutionary. It is much more respectful and sweet to call him, as Christians do, the Divine Redeemer of our souls, the Savior who frees us from the slavery of sin and demons, the Liberator who frees us from hell if we serve him faithfully.

4. That he does not flaunt having so many liberal friends, or say to others that they can do the same. Error is contagious and sticks. God addresses this in *Proverbs* (1:10): "My son, if sinners shall entice thee, consent not to them." St. Paul also says to Timothy (2 Tim. 3:5, 9), "Now these avoid...

these also resist the truth." Our holy mother Church teaches this too, and the Holy Fathers state nothing different.

Let us serve our Lord God in this world in the way that he wants us to serve him, so that we have the joy to behold, possess, and enjoy him through others. For that reason we will see one another again. So be it.

Pasto, October 29, 1897.

A.M.D.G.

Notice: *When in this little work we used phrases such as the following*: "Liberals who profess the liberalism that is condemned by the Church," *this does not mean that there are two liberalisms, one that is condemned and one that is not, one bad and the other good. We expressed things like that to accommodate the author's way of speaking, and better refute his errors. We recognize only one liberalism, which is evil, awful, and condemned by our holy mother Church.*

Third Circular

JULY 25, 1900

To the venerable secular and regular clergy of our diocese.

WE SAID IN OUR PASTORAL LETter of Lent of this year that in these days of war we have seen the appropriate righteous aversion awakened towards liberal ideas, and that the ardor has heated up Catholics to defend sane principles, even at the cost of their own lives, and that countless hearts beat to the most delicate of religious sentiments. These turn into the gentlest and tender-most expressions of the living Christian faith, into every kind of sacrifice, and into glorious heroism. Our soldiers have confirmed all of this with their Christian attitude in the last battle of the twenty-first of this month, during which everyone loudly exclaimed with consolation, "Long live the Sacred Heart of Jesus! Long live the most Blessed Virgin!" How could they not win? And they won so decisively that there is no human explanation that does not include heaven's intervention and special protection. Long live the Sacred Heart of Jesus, and long live the most Holy Virgin!

The enemies of our religion are not ignorant of the powerful driving force that moves our people to go voluntarily to the battlefields, nor of the mysterious secret that the people spread of this valor of facing hunger and exposure to the elements, of overcoming tears and loneliness for family, of generously shedding blood, of giving their lives and triumphing. It is the conviction of the sanctity of the cause that they defend, and for this the aforementioned enemies receive and then spread everywhere, with unspeakable joy, every article, whether true or false, that can put out this sacred fire that turns people into warriors and forms heroes.

We have before us a variety of such writings. They are effective at discouraging the generous and brave defenders of pure and holy beliefs. Good Catholics face harsh trials from the material. The very individuals who need to stiffen their resolve in the fight that they are conducting and in the hardships they are suffering are tempted to lose heart. The worst and most damaging are those writings with the appearance of the best of religion — prudence, charity and other virtues — that in fact condemn and bitterly reprove the determined attitude, nobility, and energy of the most avid Catholics, while offering sweet words for Lucifer's emulators. They sing hymns of triumph and hosannas to this new redeemer of theirs. Even if the sons of the world are cleverer than the sons of light, their treacherous cunning and violence would not cause so much damage if so many self-declared Catholics did not stretch out helping hands to them.

In view of this dreadful confusion that they want to introduce into everyone's thinking and that are capable of bringing dismay when we need enthusiasm and energy, I felt it necessary, venerable priests, to refute the lies that they spread and to express the Catholic truth in this short writing in a clear and simple style so that you, in turn, can explain it to the faithful of this diocese. Everyone will therefore know what they need to believe. We will signal in the headline for each paragraph the points to be addressed in relation to the errors that have been circulating at this time.

I

Falseness of a writing that is circulating

One of the writings circulating at this time with the aim of discouraging good Catholics and weakening their enthusiasm for the current battle is a fake pastoral letter from the bishop of Pamplona. This fabricated pastoral letter declares that priests *must not meddle in political affairs, nor support a particular party; that we must have charity; that our religion is a religion of peace*, and other such things in the pure liberal style that is already old and worn out from repetition. It is the work of a liberal office, and states the exact same thing that others have circulated and continue to circulate among us.

We know from seeing, through God's mercy, the animosity with which the enemies of the Church look on us that they believe that only we will call this pastoral letter apocryphal. We therefore reproduce the following circular of the Most Eminent General Vicar of the diocese of Papayán.

CIRCULAR

To the leading priests of the diocese

A manuscript entitled the *Pastoral Letter from the Bishop of Pamplona* has been widely circulated. Everyone is aware that this writing was made up by the instigators of the current revolution, with the reprehensible purpose of creating the belief that the bishop of Pamplona favors the revolution and praises the revolutionaries. As if a Catholic bishop could endorse an unjustified rebellion against the legitimate government and could praise those who profess doctrines that are condemned by the Catholic Church.

Apart from this absurdity, the falsity of this pastoral is obvious because one of the writings is attributed to Bernardo, who is the Archbishop of Bogotá. Others are attributed to Ignacio,[1] which is also not the name used by the bishop of Pamplona. Others give no name in order to avoid these errors. As well, the fabricators of this nonsense are known. Even when they have sought to imitate the style of the pastoral letters, they have used certain expressions that are not used by the bishops when they address their dioceses. This includes calling them his parishioners or his dear faithful, as how a priest speaks to his parishioners.

Everyone who believes the contents of this apocryphal writing sins by having developed poor judgment of a Catholic bishop such as the Most Eminent Parra, who has always condemned liberalism and has been persecuted as a result.

Popayán, May 18, 1900
The General Vicar

This pastoral letter is therefore apocryphal, and there is nothing more to add except that the priests are alerted to this in case they find some copies.

II

Priests should and must often get involved in politics and support a political party that is totally Catholic when it is opposed to a liberal party

As liberals never tire of repeating the same things, so we must also not become weary of giving the same answers. We have already answered the present question in chapter five of the brochure that we wrote in response to the second letter of Fr. Baltasar Vélez, and here we will

---

1   At this time, the bishop of New Pamplona, Colombia was Ignacio Antonio Parra. Perhaps he used his middle name.

reproduce this chapter, though without its introduction because that is unrelated to this issue. I said the following in that chapter:

> There is no doubt that as citizens, priests can get involved in politics without sinning, and have a higher probability of success than do many other citizens. They must get involved in politics as priests when politics attacks religion and violates sacred people and things. To stand around with folded arms while the enemies, armed with pickaxes, knock down the house of God in the political domain would be cowardice and a sin because nothing more is necessary for the enemies of the Church to triumph and achieve their aims of wrenching souls away from Catholicism and heaven and submitting them to their leader Lucifer and to hell.

We can explain these ideas themselves with clear and simple reasons, but we heard an incomparably more authoritative voice than ours on the matter. We prefer to give precedence to this voice and would like you to hear it rather than ours.

Our most holy father Leo XIII declared the following in a brief to the Archbishop of Tolosa, France, dated March 28 of last year (1897):

> We received your pastoral letter for this year's Lent, and offer congratulations for such just, moderate, and affectionate lessons that are so well adapted to the present circumstances that they give your diocese, especially in paragraph eight regarding the recommendations and teachings emanating from your supreme authority.

What does the archbishop of Tolosa say in paragraph *eight* of the pastoral letter in which he *especially congratulates* Leo XIII? He says the following:

By any chance, does the clergy not also enjoy the
same rights as other citizens? Can they not have
an opinion, interests, or even complaints, and
therefore aspire to get representatives who advocate for their grievances? Certainly, we would be
very grateful to limit our political expressions
to singing the *Te Deum* for the victories of the
fatherland and performing the funeral rites for
their famous dead, to recommending from the
pulpit the prayers of the people for the head of
state, and to intoning with total precision the
Domine, salvam fac Rempublicam. But this is not
possible due to the fierce hatred with which we
are pursued and the unceasing work that they
do to legally destroy the influence of religion
on the country.

The duties of Catholics have changed just as
the situation has changed. Are we in reality the
sort to be preoccupied with politics? Is it not, in
contrast, politics that is preoccupied, with ill-will,
with us, who spy on our gatherings and inquire
into our statements in order to incriminate us?

How can they noisily discuss in the press,
political reunions, and deliberative assemblies,
and raise against our interests the gravest questions of Church-state relations, the liberty of the
apostolic ministry, the education of youth, the
issue of religious congregations, and the moral
future of the country, while we do without our
own press, public gatherings, and deliberative
assemblies? Are we to receive all the knocks
without saying a word, and to resign ourselves
to the role of the disenfranchised in our own
country under the pretext that the reign of Jesus
Christ is not of this world? Even though he is
not of this world, he is destined to operate over
this world and is intimately connected to it. He
possesses external and public institutions that
in all their points are connected with human

institutions. This reign develops and spreads out in time and space, and it is essential that it does so in freedom.

It is repeated over and over: *Give to Caesar that which is Caesar's!* But when Caesar usurps that which is not his, when he invades the domain of the Lord and oppresses consciences, we have the right to resist him legally and the duty to represent him and his injustice respectfully but firmly. We have the right to convince him and say to him, as the Savior said to the servant of the high priest when he slapped him, *Why did you hit me? Quid me caedes?*

These practical necessities are so clearly evident that wherever political will reigns, in other words, in almost all of the civilized world, Catholics use this liberty in defense of the interests of their faith. In effect, they form *an organized party*, send their candidates to parliament, make alliances, negotiate with power, set out their conditions, and direct public negotiations with the *character of a party*. The clergy participates in elections directly and actively almost everywhere except in France.

Along with our holy father Leo XIII, we congratulate the archbishop of Tolosa for these teachings. In these congratulations and teachings we must take to heart those who dare to state that *priests must not get involved in politics*. The clergy *can get involved* in politics, and even *must get involved* in politics, on occasions like those noted by the archbishop of Toloso, that is, when it is in the interest of the Church. We believe, however, that when politics is just, and respects and practices the teachings of our holy mother the Church, *generally* speaking, it is best that priests do not get involved in politics.

That was the chapter that we wrote two years ago. It is enough to prove what we proposed with this point. We add, however, what the Most Eminent Cardinal Guibert stated to Mr. Grévy, president of the French Republic in a letter dated March 30, 1886. "How can anyone condemn the fact that the clergy prefer those who protect them to those who dispossess them, those who honor their ministry to those who discredit it, those who support the influence of religion in souls to those who do everything to destroy it?" No, it is not possible to reproach this conduct. It is so clear and obvious that there is no one who does not understand and confess that this is how it must be, except for those who have an interest in understanding this situation differently.

III

The non-intervention principle and the union of good Catholics to defend the kingdom of Jesus Christ everywhere

No one who is moderately instructed in religious matters is unaware that one of the propositions (no. 62) that the Church condemns in the *Syllabus* is the following: "*The* non-intervention *principle must be proclaimed and observed.*" Pius IX already condemned this principle in his address *Novos et ante* of September 28, 1860.

Périn[2] notes, "Modern theories of *non-intervention* are the logical consequence of the principles of free law. They tend to make it impossible to attack the liberty of evil. They hide their true objective, which is to support the revolution in its work of social destruction, under the guise of humanitarian respect for the right of people to independence and the principle of nationalities. They do not worry themselves with the revolution, which is inconsequential, as long as they reach their goals. While they hold firm in their code to the supposed principle of

---

2   Charles Périn (1815–1905), Belgian economist and professor for national economy at the Catholic University of Louvain.

non-intervention, they have proudly violated this many times whenever it served their objectives. But they have energetically demanded its application every time they have encountered either a way to destroy society's inner ordering through the collapse of legitimate authorities, or a way to disturb the international order with the adoption of a new right."

If Périn were among us to witness the conduct of Ecuador's revolutionary government in these months, he could not have given a more precise portrait of this conduct as that which appears in the cited paragraph. And yet, the mystery of it all! For despite this conduct and the church's condemnation against the *non-intervention* principle, Mr. Carlos Cuervo Márquez, minister of exterior relations of a government that calls itself Catholic, had no scruple in uniting his voice with that of Mr. L. J. Carbo, a minister of Ecuador, in condemning the contrary of what the Church condemns. He confessed, in other words, a doctrine that is completely the opposite of what can be found in an official document of the Church. And he did so in a bold and shameless way that includes these words of the above-mentioned minister: "We condemn the politics of intervention as disastrous and dangerous for America."

We protest with all the powers of our soul, and in our nature as a Catholic bishop, against this minister's condemnation. The authors of the proposition that is condemned in the *Syllabus* do not dare to say so much. They are more restrained. They do not apply the descriptions used by the ministers of the famous agreement of June 15 that was broken by Alfaro with the battalions of his regular army when he struck Colombian territory. He used cannons to fire at our valiant, tough, and heroic Christian soldiers of the southern villages. They were abandoned to themselves, starving and exposed, and had few or poor arms. Yet they ably faced up to the forces that the revolutionary government of Ecuador sent to support the Colombian revolutionaries.

The principle of *non-intervention* can be reasonable in a normal situation in which it is faithfully applied and taken in the sense that each nation must arrange its own matters without the interference of other nations, as required by independence. However, as already stated, the revolution seeks something else. The revolution, as it confesses, does not recognize frontiers, and pursues the principle that all legitimate authorities and Catholic governments are defenseless against its attacks. In this way it can gain access and dominate everywhere.

Given the revolution's cosmopolitan nature and the fact that it is organized in every way to wage war against Our Lord Jesus Christ and all that belongs to him, the counter-revolution that it is the duty of Catholics to wage must also be cosmopolitan. Everyone from everywhere must also be united to defend Jesus Christ, Lord and King, not only as individuals, but as collectivities, either in the form of fractions, as with states or nations, or under a generic name understood by society. The sovereignty of Jesus Christ is not limited to one nation, but extends to everyone because the Father gave all of them to him as an inheritance. They all belong to him by right of acquisition, because he gave himself for the recovery of all. He won everyone away from the darkness. This right of Jesus Christ to rule over every part logically corresponds to our duty to do whatever we can so that he reigns, not here and there, but everywhere.

In order to work for greater success for the social reign of Jesus Christ, it is obvious that Catholics need to be linked with closer ties than those which connect the enemies that enable them to attack and destroy this reign. Regarding this, St. Thomas distinguishes two classes of union. One, we can call of the flesh. It has the objective of committing evil. This is the union of these men who attempt to corrupt, pervert, de-Catholicize, and wage war against Jesus Christ and his Church, ministers, and whoever belongs to him.

The Sacred Doctor called the other union the union of the spirit. This is what true Catholics form. Its objective is to obtain the reign of Jesus Christ in all things, in such a way, that he is honored in private and public life, in the church and streets, in laws and customs, and in every social organism of all nations. Against the universal union of all the enemies of Jesus Christ made to wage war and take down his reign, the union of the friends of Jesus Christ is a necessity for defending his sovereignty and upholding his reign in every region and in everything.

IV

A false spirit of reconciliation appeared
these days among us against the union
and action of good Catholics

Today, with so much progress and advancement, many people do not think as in the past. Many have become compliant. They have made themselves nicer and opened themselves to such a wide base of attraction that they think it is now normal to have friendships with high-ranking masons and to accept with so many kind words men who hate Jesus Christ to death. This adulation and affability has developed to such an extent that they would have stated to the glorious St. Ignatius of Loyola that he should have rectified his conduct and withdrawn his beautiful letter that states that we must regard heresy with horror as a sign of love for Jesus Christ, and would also have said to sacred authors that they need to correct the *nec Ave dixeritis*, and the *cum his nec cibum sumere*, and many others such as these, and even stronger than these.

It has been noted that there has been a wholehearted attempt by some to get people to stop thinking so badly about the enemies of Jesus Christ, and to cease working with such intransigence against the things they do.

A few wanted us to reconcile and unite with the revolutionary government of Ecuador even while this government was unloading its cannons against our heroic Christian soldiers, undoubtedly to pull the strings of our Catholic hearts, which were frayed by this. They condemned the doctrines that our holy mother Church supports in the boldest manner. They also showed that the governments of Colombia and Ecuador have friendly feelings of mutual reinforcement, even brotherhood, and even added that *fortunately there is agreement in ideas and purposes between the two governments.*

Our Lord God permitted the revolutionary government of Ecuador to answer these extreme and incredible treasures with its regular troops' cannons and battalions that it launched against Colombia. If the battalions of the revolutionary government of Ecuador had not given much to the government of Colombia, we believe that this is due *only* to God, who did not want to see our Christian soldiers humiliated. They had prepared for combat with the reception of the sacraments and prayers to God about the battles. God therefore had mercy on these people who adored, implored, hoped in, and confessed him in front of men.

But is it true that the government of Colombia had friendly feelings, and not any kind of friendly feelings, but those *of brotherhood*, with the revolutionary and *masonic* government of Ecuador? Would it not cause a scandal to call a mason *brother*?[3] And is it also true that *fortunately there exists agreement in ideas and propositions of both governments*? In what ways is our government in agreement

---

3 Masons call each other *brother*.

with the ideas and purposes of the revolutionary and masonic government of Ecuador? We have to find that out. If it is in the manner of governing people, we must protest with all the energy of our soul against these ideas and propositions. We believe that we can do this in the name of all our clergy and good Catholics of the diocese. No, as Catholics we do not want nor cannot want this agreement of ideas and purposes with masons and liberals.

If the agreement of ideas refers only to the way of acknowledging the successes that took place on this frontier, we cannot turn our backs on the most notable Catholic citizens of the population. We unite our voice to that of the beloved dioceses that represent the Most Excellent President of the republic and say to him that the celebrated pact is *depressing to the national honor and is notoriously unjust with the loyal and self-sacrificing defenders of the legitimacy and integrity of the fatherland in these remote regions.* The invasion of the regular troops of Alfaro on the 21st of this month, in union with the Colombian revolutionaries, gave reason to those who have it and completely confused those who pledge themselves to see us as liberal and masonic brothers.

Thanks to God and due to the backgrounds and conduct of the men who today occupy the high positions in the nation, they promise to work in a different way. We hope that they think and speak as pure and clear Catholics and that they properly represent the *national faith*, which is Catholic, apostolic, and Roman, and which is defended today so ardently and valiantly by the army which at the same time defends the country and government.

Others joined up with the senior ministers of the famous pact that was broken by Alfaro's cannons when the ink of the signatures had not yet dried. They also yelled: "Why do you have so much hate and vilification for some of our brothers only because they have this or that political marking?" That's what those who wrote the apocryphal pastoral letter ask. As if he was touched in his soul when reading this, a priest stated in another writing, as if continuing the thought: "We need to stretch out our hands in friendship to everyone else, bathed in light and mercy."

In other words, in order to please these men, we need to correct the Sacred Scriptures and the works of the Church Fathers and Doctors of the Church in those passages that do not treat the enemies of God gently. The Catholic world will have to repeal the label *Doctor Mellifluus* to St. Bernard himself because he called Arnaldo de Brescia the "seductor, vessel of insults, scorpion, cruel wolf." It is enough, and ought to be enough, that Our Lord Jesus Christ calls Herod a *fox* and the Jews a *wicked and adulterous generation, bleached sepulchers, hypocrites, sons of the devil.*

We can disregard, then, certain voices, and these voices should not have any power to undo the union of good Catholics, nor to lead us astray with tenderness, compromise, and reconciliation with the enemies of our Lord Jesus Christ. A modern French apologist notes, "To measure the friendship of Paul for Peter, do not only ask how Paul treated Peter. Ask how Paul treated Peter's enemies. There is the secret." The same apologist stated, "The saint who appears in the world today should have a sweet charity that blesses anyone and anything for any occasion. The saint that the world imagines would smile at error, sin, at everyone and everything. He would be good, kind, and sickeningly sweet with the ill and indulgent with sickness. If you want to be such a saint, the world will love you and say that in this way you make Christianity loved."

It seems to us that it is a perfect painter who has made this portrait of what many wish Catholics would be. It is a perfect portrait from a master.

To conclude this point, we recall that our holy father Leo XIII condemned *Americanism*, which has the following foundation: "To more easily attract dissidents to Catholic truth, the Church must adapt to the civilization of a world that has progressed by ceding its ancient rigor and expressing reconciliation in accordance with the aspirations and demands of modern people." The Holy Father condemns Americanism in order to *protect the integrity of the faith and to keep watch over the salvation of souls*. It is, then, a very serious condemnation, and those calling for reconciliation must take it into account.

V

A false patriotism which has also appeared at this time is shaking the union of Catholics

A thousand curses on patriotism that prefers the country to religion. Another thousand curses on patriotism that says that the country is the religion, and object of worship, and everything, as we can read in one of the writings that is circulating! What damage this false patriotism causes the country and religion!

As stated above, no one can doubt the desirability and necessity of the union of good Catholics of all parts to form a more beneficial opposition to the enemies of our Lord Jesus Christ. Those enemies also unite from all over to wage war and achieve their satanic plans. For this reason, we looked on with so much pleasure at the brotherhood, and at the affection, harmony, and unity that around here exists between Catholics of different nationalities. We hope for the beautiful and beneficial results from this union that will help the Catholic cause. The greatest benefit of this is not the abstract and theoretical defense of doctrines. It is the uniting and assisting of those who set these doctrines out in the practical terrain and the combatting of whoever opposes the realization of these in the practical terrain. Bad doctrines do not damage the Church much if these only remain in the theoretical realm, and there is no one to defend them in the practical terrain or to spread them by the sword. For this we must oppose arguments with arguments, the party with a party, unity with unity, and bayonets with bayonets.

Anyone can understand this. That's why we endeavor to make Catholics understand this. But just as there was an attempt to introduce a false spirit of reconciliation with evil among us in order to undo this union of Catholics that was forming, so also was there an attempt to introduce a false patriotism with the same goal.

This false patriotism imputed to our brave Christian soldiers low and reprehensible things, and went so far in its atheistic extreme to express fear that brought about the total ruin of the neighboring nation. If this was about masons and liberals, about those who hold *free opinions*, about those with *free consciences* that allow for the committing of every type of injustice, the fear would be understandable. But this is clearly about Catholic soldiers who frequently go to confession and receive communion, soldiers who enter combat with the cry, *long live Jesus Christ!*, and who have no other aim but that Jesus Christ lives and reigns everywhere. It is these soldiers who are feared as the total ruin of nations. It is not the enemies of God who are thus feared, which would not be strange, but those who call themselves Catholics! Overwhelmed by this fear, they sound the cry of alarm, and inflame those filled with a false and lethal patriotism that divides Catholic against Catholic and encourages and raises the spirits of the enemies of God.

How true it is that we so often sacrifice religion for the fatherland. This damages both! There are such men who confess to being great and enthusiastic patriots who cannot patiently bear the name *foreigner*, even regarding those things that are related to religion. The false patriotism of these men impedes them from considering and seeing that the word *foreigner* lacks any sense, strictly speaking, when applied to religious things, and that, furthermore, with this conduct they prioritize the country over religion, which harms both.

The unity of faith and hierarchy forms Catholics into a single people. On the day of the magnificent rebirth in the Upper Room with the descent of the Holy Spirit, there was already no difference between Jew and Roman, barbarian and Greek, and now we have to make it less between English and French, African and Asian, Colombian and Ecuadorian. We must not divide Catholics with such concepts as territorial frontiers, but instead with morals and doctrine. A Colombian atheist or liberal, for example, must be more foreign for good Catholic Colombians than a foreigner who is a good Catholic from the furthest reaches of Oceania.

This false patriotism that prefers country to religion harms both, as mentioned. For example, those who cannot hide their dislike for worthy foreign priests and vowed religious cause harm, no matter how much good these foreigners do. The false patriotism of these men repels the good services that the foreigners could give souls and religion. This causes incalculable harm to the very country that the false patriots claim to love so much. We cite this example and can point out others.

Catholics! Don't listen to what false patriotism tells you. Continue in your union, in your mutual affection, in close love and affectionate brotherhood based on the unity of beliefs, on Christian charity, and on the desire to see Jesus Christ reign everywhere. Those who condemn this friendship, brotherhood, and unity, remember the condemnation of the following thesis: *The evangelical teaching that calls for brothers to help each other mutually is only for individuals and cannot be applied to political relations in support of legitimate governments who are unjustly attacked by interior or exterior enemies.* This thesis is the eighth out of a group of theses denounced by the Holy See. They merit theological censure for *harming society, sedition, destruction of public and citizen rights, and heresy.* The opposite doctrine, then, is the true teaching of the Church.

VI

The faith can and must be defended on the battlefield

It is difficult to believe that we see the necessity to ask this simple and clear question that has been resolved for the humblest Christians, but that these days is shouted from the battle camps: "We want to defend our holy religion." Although the question is so clear and settled by the Catholic sense of the faithful, the documents that are currently circulating force us to bring it up because those who write these articles think that our soldiers, who defend the faith on the battlefield, commit a horrendous crime and should put down their arms and march back home.

"Peace, peace!" cry out all the documents that are circulating these days that we have in view. The apocryphal pastoral letter declares, "Our religion is peace. Our Lord Jesus Christ preached peace and gave us an example of it. Why, then, should we contribute to the war and encourage it?"

"We must work for peace," another article states. "Let us love peace and work for its reign."

"Let us keep peace and perfect friendship," the ministers of the famous pact also declare. "Fortunately, there is agreement on ideas and purposes."

Another states: "No more fighting in the name of a religion of charity and peace."

Still another: "Avoiding war at all costs is very appropriate for our status for the present circumstances."

Another: "The Christian religion is peaceful. The saber and the rifle is unnecessary for establishing and spreading it through the whole world. Neither is war necessary now to preserve it."

The Church's enemies have distributed these documents in great numbers. They pose no little temptation to our soldiers to lay down their arms. Thanks to God, they had received instructions and encouragement and were ready to keep fighting.

It really is the time to say with Holy Scripture, *Pax, pax, et non erat pax*. Peace, peace, they say to us and shout. At the same time, they shoot at us and wage a cruel and unjust war even when it is costly for them.

The peace that they preach is apparently only applied to Catholics. They must keep the peace, sit back, and let the liberals dominate, steal, slap others in the face, and kill. Because they have *free consciences*, they can do these things. If liberals and masons expected this, if they imagine that our soldiers would answer their cannon shots with a sermon from the chaplains about Christian meekness, they have already seen that they have tricked themselves. They have seen, and not only once but many times, that our soldiers, these soldiers who pray and prepare themselves for combat with confession and communion, know how to make their strikes hit back hard, and not only hit the air.

In fighting for their religion in the way that they did, our soldiers fulfilled a duty. A people can and must defend the truth faith that is in its possession against every type of enemy that wants to disturb it. True faith is the most precious honor that a people can have. They can and must conserve it at all costs, and even with arms if this is necessary.

The true faith is worth more than a nation's territorial integrity. It is worth more than the honor of the national flag. It is worth more than the fatherland itself in its entirety, because without faith it is impossible to please God and to achieve the ultimate end in eternity. Without the fatherland, one can still please God and achieve the ultimate end. If, then, it is possible to wage war for the territorial integrity of the fatherland, to redress an assault on the national honor, or for other just motives, how much more is it permissible to fight for the true faith, which is worth more than all of that? Either we have the right to fight in this case, or in no case at all.

Our good Catholics speak rightly when they declare, "We are going to defend our holy religion." They do the right thing when they go to the leaders and ask for a rifle to defend it from those who attack it with rifles. They are doing nothing different from so many Christian soldiers who fought for their faith against the Moors and heretics. Did the Church not bless the expeditions of the crusaders? In modern times, did Pope Pius IX not bless the bayonets of the pontifical Zouaves?

Let us not be seduced by an exaggerated love for peace and leniency to the point where we create true deserters of the beautiful Catholic standard. Sometimes the term "peace" is used for things that are not of peace and that are even complicit with hell. This is why when the enemy makes so many cries of "peace, peace," the warrior cries of our valiant Catholics, in defense of religion, sound so pleasant.

When we see Jesus Christ treated as an intruder and cast out from the protection of the law, from centers of instruction, and from all parts of the neighboring nation by an impious government; when we see that this government is pleased to dictate laws that enslave the free and beautiful Spouse of Jesus Christ, the Church; when we see this government attack our territory with its battalions, brandishing satanic banners in union with the revolutionaries of Colombia, intending to establish over our people the reign of Lucifer; when we see that they want to carry out this great mystery of iniquity and attack, hurt, and kill us, and nothing more only because they cannot, how—great God!—how can we preach peace? No, peace is not possible. In this case, peace is betrayal and apostasy. In these circumstances, there is nothing else but the cry of war, the cry of Julius II: "OUT WITH THE BARBARIANS!" The cry of the crusaders is the same as that which we hear these days from our fervent and valiant Catholics: Let us fight for our religion! GOD WILLS IT!

VII

Conclusion

So many and dangerous are the errors contained in the writings that are passed so quickly from hand to hand these days in the places of our diocese that it was necessary to speak and fulfill our duty. We spoke to drive out the discouragement, weakness, and disquiet that these writings can cause in a time that requires determination, energy, valor, and all the enthusiasm that the sanctity of the cause that we defend requires.

Of all the errors that were spread, we have exposed and fought only the most dangerous, that is, only those covered in the beautiful attire of truth and virtue. We did not mention the other great errors that are found in these writings because they are so noticeable, absurd, and clear that they cannot do much damage. The simplest of the faithful exposed, rejected, and condemned them with only the instruction of the catechism.

The evils that afflict the Church today are not primarily caused by great unbelievers, impious, or persecutors. The work of these imitators of Lucifer would be mostly sterile without the work of the conciliators. The conciliators say that the determined fight against evil is *intransigence*. They have undoubtedly forgotten this sentence from the Savior: *Whoever is not with me is against me*. Yes, the greatest dangers that truth and virtue face today are not from great and scandalous heretics, but from the falsification of virtue and truth. The more skilled these falsifications are, the more they seduce and endanger.

It is understandable that certain men who want and seek ministries of the altar are accommodating, flexible, and wise according to the flesh. But nowadays some are fatally deceived in believing that they work for the good of the Church by ceding a little to its enemies. They employ clear language and accommodating phrases, and later walk arm and arm with them to applause. Avoid this behavior, eminent co-workers, for God's glory, for your honor, and for the good of souls so that you can be certain that when the day of revolution comes, the shrewd ringleader will laugh at and scorn those who serve him or ask for favor or grace in some way. It is an error, and an unfortunate error for the Church and for souls, to give in to the enemies of Jesus Christ and to softly and complacently go with them. More damage has been done to Jesus's Church through cowardice disguised as prudence and moderation than through the furious cries and strikes of impiety.

Take from it the good that you can! Avoid greater evils! These are two of the formulas that, applied to the issue under consideration, produce the contrary effects. At times, they are nothing more than pretexts for covering up fear and cowardice. This does not allow for a dignified attitude. What has ever been achieved with gentleness and flirtation with the enemies of Jesus Christ? What evils, big or small, have ever been avoided with these paths? Nothing has ever been achieved with this conduct aside from strengthening the power of evil, calming—oh, what pain!—the holy wrath that men must feel towards heresy and error. The faithful become accustomed to seeing with a certain indifference these persecutions of the Church. This leads even to fatalism, as they say, "It is good the way it is." What war or what evil would be worse for the people than this evil?

Beloved co-workers of ours, avoid, I repeat, this disastrous conduct. Avoid it for the love of God, and also for the love of your own soul and those of your neighbors. Teach the people the doctrines that we explained about the errors that the enemies of God have been currently circulating, and encourage the faithful so that they continue the fight as they have until now. Encourage the union of all Catholics, which is so important, and take care that they love each other as brothers, regardless of their nation. No less important is complete separation from liberals. The two armies can be clearly demarcated from each other by the two flags. On the one side are those who recognize and adore Jesus Christ, King of kings and absolute Lord of souls, peoples, and nations. On the other side are those who loathe, wage war against, and expel him as an intruder and thief of the laws, institutions, and government of the peoples.

Reverend priests, you must understand perfectly that there cannot be peace, but only war, between the two armies. Those who preach peace between these two armies preach the impossible. Peace is not possible as long as one of the two armies does not cede. We cannot cede because that would be a criminal and horrendous apostasy. While they do not cede, peace is impossible. We can only have war.

Catholics! Together fight the Lord's battles and march united into combat. Forward! For Jesus Christ, who will give us victory! For his divine Heart, who has protected us so visibly! For the most holy Virgin in her glorious titles of Virgin of Mercy and Las Lajas, who has shown herself so favorably and lovingly! Catholics! Soldiers of the faith! Let us not make ourselves unworthy by committing an evil while under the extraordinary protection that heaven has shown us until now. Let us give glory to God in all moments and places. Whoever suffers for Jesus Christ is a confessor of Jesus Christ! Whoever finds his bliss by dying for Jesus Christ will be a martyr of Jesus Christ! A joyous, happy, enviable death!

Long live the unity of all Catholics
in, with, and for Jesus Christ!
Let us fight for the defense of our
religion! Jesus Christ wills it!

Long live Jesus Christ!
✝ Fr. Ezequiel, *Bishop of Pasto.*

APPENDIX

Funeral Homily

PREACHED IN THE CATHEDRAL OF
PASTO BY THE MOST REVEREND
EZEQUIEL MORENO DÍAZ, FOR THE
FUNERARY HONORS FOR THE SOUL
OF THE MOST REVEREND DR. D.
PETER SCHUMACHER, BISHOP OF
PORTOVIEJO ON AUGUST 9, 1902.

Et per illam defunctus adhuc loquitur.
He being dead yet speaketh.
Heb. 11:4.

My beloved children in Christ:

WE FIND OURSELVES IN THE
presence of a tomb that recalls to us a
man who no longer lives, and still does
live; a man who disappeared from among the living,
and still lives; a man who is dead, and still speaks.
Who is he?

He is one of the most select of the ministers of Jesus
Christ, who trained many others who today are decorated in the ornaments of Catholicism by their learning
and virtues. He is a prelate full of brotherly love who
did much good for others. He is a bishop who was
jealous of the rights of the Church of Jesus Christ. He
is a staunch defender of the Catholic faith. He is even
more. He is a distinguished confessor of this divine faith
without which it is impossible to please God; this faith
that is your faith, mine, that of all the good; this faith

213

that is unspoilt, pure, without mixture. His faith is a faith that saves individuals, peoples, and nations. Today such a faith is unfortunately rare.

Who is this prelate, this bishop, this defender of the faith? Everyone knows. He is the Most Reverend D. Pedro Schumacher, the most dignified bishop of Portoviejo. He will justly appear in the history of this country as wise, hardworking, virtuous, vigorous, heroic, generous, and a thousand more entirely praiseworthy designations.

Naturally, I had inscribed on his tomb the greatest epitaph that St. Paul wrote to pay homage to the faith of Abel: *Et per illam defunctus adhuc loquitur.* Msgr. Schumacher is dead. Yet he still speaks through the faith, through this faith, for which he fought throughout his whole life until his last moment and suffered slander, insults, work, and harsh banishment.

My task is so sad! In recent days I have asked many people the following question: "Whom should I appoint for the funeral address of the Most Reverend Bishop Schumacher?" No one gave any answer other than the following: "Your Excellency must do it." This unanimous reply gives me reason to draw your attention to the memory of the great bishop of Portoviejo. But I assure you that I hide his brilliance and that there are so many flowers of great worth on his crown that I do not know which to choose. I have to leave out many, and many good ones. It is not possible to say everything. In this need to leave much out, I will stay with what I think to be the most significant. I will show you his virtues in his office of bishop and, after reflecting on these, we will contemplate one in particular, but contemplate it separately because it is deserving. This is his strength in defending the faith.

You already know my theme. I formulate it in this proposition: "The pastoral virtues of the Most Reverend

D. Pedro Schumacher, especially his strength in defending the integrity of the faith, made him the bishop that the Catholic Church needed in these times."

Now, put yourselves in my place and penetrate the sentiments of my soul, so that you can be lenient if my heart speaks more and better than my tongue.

Great God! Do not allow me to profane this place with unmerited praise, nor let me part from you, who are the eternal Truth.

The plan that I have made obliges me to pass in silence over the infancy of the Most Reverend Schumacher, his education in the faith, his studies, his generous detachment from the world and embrace of the Institute of the great St. Vincent de Paul, and his brilliant explanations, exquisite wisdom, and good name in the centers of teaching where his superiors placed him.

With pain I avoid these beautiful things, things from which could come many brilliant words of praise. This includes considering him adorned with the miter, as a wise and virtuous Lazarist in 1885; following him to Portoviejo, where he entered in August of the same year; and studying him in the midst of his sons while carrying out his great duties.

Open yourselves, doors of the seminary in Quito. Open yourselves, however sensitive the departure is for the soul of discipline and fervor. Open yourselves, even though it causes the pain of separation of direction, master, and the support of everyone. Open yourselves to make way for the man who is needed in Manabi and assert the interests of religion.

Oh, what a happy day it was for Portoviejo when it received its bishop, the Most Reverend D. Pedro Schumacher! Let us enter with him into his diocese to admire him.

I

His Pastoral Virtues

The episcopacy did not alter in any way the life of prayer and virtue, study and teaching, work and actions of the humble son of St. Vincent de Paul. On the contrary, he found many ways to exercise his ministry in the diocese of Portoviejo, in Manabi, where so much was lacking and needed to be done. I do not wish to say what this diocese needed. For my good luck, and yours, the deceased spoke always of it, as I mentioned to you. Listen to what was in a pastoral letter that he wrote in the month that he arrived in Portoviejo, the only one of his that I have. Unfortunately, I could not find any more to inspire me for this occasion:

> Although the next morning is not certain, we did not hesitate to lay the foundation of the establishment of education, from which we promise great and valuable results for Catholic and social life in our diocese...We have the satisfaction to say that the seminary college will be opening in a few weeks. The boys and teenagers will find there the means for acquiring a literary career and following academic courses... We have not lost the view of the state and condition of teaching in the primary schools. We will not hesitate to communicate the means that we are preparing to help primary school teachers... We have turned to the Congregation of the Sisters of Charity. The favorable response that we have received gives us hope for such powerful help for the education of girls and young women... Meanwhile, we have received delegates from many parts of our diocese which, in moving ways, petition us for priests... Moved by the desire to look after this, we have determined to seek priests... At the same time, we continue to prepare for the arrival

of missionaries and more priests who will fill
the vacancies in the clergy that we currently
have in our diocese.

The Most Reverend Schumacher did or planned all
of this in his month of arrival in the diocese. Who is
not amazed by this and does not see in this the kind of
bishop that the Church needs in these times? The diocese
had great needs, but it had a bishop with a magnanimous
heart to fill them.

After a few years had passed since the Most Reverend Schumacher's arrival to Manabi, the region's inhabitants could already say with stirring joy to outsiders:
"See these schools governed by intelligent and virtuous
religious who have come from France, Germany, Switzerland, and the United States? They were founded by
the Most Reverend Schumacher. See these schools filled
with children? They were encouraged and taken by the
Most Reverend Schumacher. See those people governed
by an educated and virtuous clergy? They were trained
by the Most Reverend Schumacher. See the most iso-
lated and unhealthy towns and hamlets, instructed by
zealous missionaries? The Most Reverend Schumacher
brought them. See Christian customs, piety, devotion, and
frequent reception of the sacraments? This is the work
of the Most Reverend Schumacher. See this beautiful
church, this elegant building, this magnificent bridge, this
convenient path? The Most Illustrious Schumacher built
them. Do you see? But where am I going with this? That
is enough to show that the Most Reverend Schumacher
was a bishop whom the Church needed in these times.
Now hear new evidence for this truth.

The loftiness of his ministry penetrated our bishop. He
applied himself with perseverance to the persecution of
errors and vices, knowing that the treatment of profound
and inveterate afflictions is not the work of a single day.

It was said in Rome when Christianity came there, "The gods have no place here." "Errors and vice have no place here," said thinking people when the Most Reverend Schumacher came to Manabi, and they saw him work. Those who thought like that, thought well. They asked this bishop to go out and make his business the business of faith, sacrifices, penalties, constancy, and heroism. Everything was his to do, and he could put everything into practice to work for the beneficial changes that we desired and sought. He visited his diocese without letting the fierce sun, hard ground, or torrential rain stop him from his unceasing eagerness for the good of everyone. With the light of his doctrine, he taught the science of Jesus Christ. The power of his example made virtue lovable. He used the power of anathema against rebels and the scandalous, imitating the apostle for whom the body is nothing, as long as the soul be saved.

These virtues, however, would have come to nothing without charity. Was the great bishop lacking in this beautiful virtue? No. He had the virtue of charity, and at a very high level. Oh! The stones themselves will speak of the charity of the Most Reverend Schumacher if no one else will. But everyone speaks of this charity. The places where he came and did good deeds speak of it. The poor, to whom he gave his very own poor food, speak of it. The sick, treated in his own house, speak of it. A thousand needy, who were helped by his great love, speak of it. Samaniego! You were a witness every day of the beautiful scene of a bishop preparing remedies for the sick and curing the disgusting ulcers with his consecrated hands!

After the Most Reverend was banished from his diocese due to the impious, he found a way to keep practicing his apostolic virtues in exile. We all saw him poor, submissive, pious, loving, sweet, and humble. He fled the noise of the world and dedicated himself to the salvation of souls.

Yascual, Guachavez, Samaniego, Linares, towns that were all made fruitful by his apostolic works, give us an account of his fruitful missions, fervent general communions, wise counsels, sweet manner, tenderness, and charity! Oh! Dear towns! Why do I ask you? Not so that you answer. You can only weep for the loss of such a great good.

You who are disbelievers due to fashion, vanity, or caprice! You who have a thousand times shown your tongues to be full of venom, hearts full of hate, and souls full of boldness against the pleasant, sweet, and charitable Reverend D. Pedro Schumacher: Go to Manabi and examine his works without prejudice. Go to Samaniego and ask what he did. Calmly listen to what these people say of the one you persecute and slander. You will hear enthusiastic blessings and praise. No, he did not die forgotten and abandoned. He died surrounded by grateful hearts who cried and will cry for their father and benefactor. He died dear to and respected by all the faithful sons of the Church. He died with the glorious fame of having been the bishop that the Church in this time needed.

But time flies, and it is already necessary to contemplate, alone and separately, the virtue that we all saw as most illuminated in our bishop.

II

His fortitude in defending the integrity of the Catholic faith

The tribute that I make to this exceptional virtue of the Most Reverend D. Pedro Schumacher would be pale if I were only inspired by my short understanding. But I can seek these inspirations in his writings, in the characteristics of his feather. I will seek as much as I can in those. Listen, of course, to some of these characteristics that certain actions allow us to see. This knowledge is necessary to better assess his strength. *Defunctus adhuc loquitur*: the deceased still speaks in a piece of writing that he wrote in 1896 in which he writes,

> It was about five years ago when, on the occasion of political elections, ominous shouts were heard for the first time: 'Down with the cassocks! Death to friars!' The venerable bishop of Loja[1] understood at that moment where the savvy enemy was going, and gave the members of his diocese the alert.... He of course knew what the masons intended. They later shouted, 'Down with Christ!' There were at that time certain blind and flaccid Catholics who did not want to recognize in these rallies the test or advance guard of masonry that was carefully though decisively moving ahead. Even a minister of state bitterly complained to me that I had reminded the duty of the public authority to punish these blasphemers ... Masonry taught and guided some people on how to insult priests. Liberalism, accomplice and ally of such a devilish undertaking, advised the pastors of the Church to keep silent. From this same time, the liberal press was overflowing with heresy and Voltarian sarcasm, like Ecuador had never seen. The bishops did not hesitate to complain. Ecuadorian laws explicitly ordered punishment to the impious press. But, *for the sake of moderation*, it was all left as was. To pacify and desensitize Catholics and favor the work of the masons, propositions like the following are repeated at higher levels: 'In Ecuador we are all Catholics. There are no dissidents. Those who are bothered and have fear are over-reactors, stubborn, and fanatics.' Encouraged by this tolerance, impiety passed from words to actions. The Church and religion were sacrificed in the attempt to avoid any fuss with liberal theory.

---

1   Monsignor José Ramón Masiá, OFM (1815–1902).

So speaks the deceased. These are all his words. The flood of impiety, against which he fought in defending the integrity of the faith, cannot be made clearer than that. He also lets us know that he not only opposed this flood of evil with his teachings, but also raised his voice against the supreme power of the nation in order to restrain evil there. He pointed his finger at the truly guilty, who are lax and moderate Catholics who tolerated impiety. They let liberalism progress and build enough energy to climb the ladder of power and begin to practice the degenerative, antichristian, and antisocial principles of liberalism while governing the people.

If Jesus Christ no longer reigns in many nations, the truly guilty are liberal Catholics and individuals who are savvy about, tolerant of, and mild with liberalism. Such a horrible sin! It is the great sin of the time. The Most Reverend Schumacher pointed this sin out. He condemned and fought against it. This provided a valuable service to Catholicism and society. He showed himself to be the bishop that the Church needed in these times.

The Most Reverend Schumacher knew perfectly well that the Church teaches that Catholicism cannot reconcile or make any compromises with liberalism. The experienced bishop was convinced that a concession to error, however small, really amounted to taking a new position and a new advance for a close-up attack against the truth. It meant doing much damage to it.

The zealous prelate had evidence that all compromise, capitulation, appeasement, and mildness with error give victory to the revolution in a cowardly way. It lacks the resistance or fight that is our obligation, since victory depends on God.

It was not hidden from the wise pastor that there can be no peace between error and truth, and not even neutral territory. He saw that wherever error and truth meet, battle is necessary and unavoidable because it is impossible that they unite and mix, just as it is impossible for light and darkness to unite and mix. The darkness dissipates as the light grows. The two can never walk hand-in-hand. This is just as true for the truth, which is light, as for error, which is darkness. The Most Reverend Schumacher knew all of this as the clear truth that the past teaches us. At this point, this teaching is the history of the present and will be the history of the future.

He knew all of this because not a few nations are living and unimpeachable testimonies that prove these truths, just as today there are nations where these truths are taught, and where they are taken to be exaggerations and stubbornness.

He knew all of this because, in addition to having studied, attentively and in depth the great political-religious question that shook the world, he saw, felt, and touched what the events themselves taught.

For the same reason that he understood all that, he never ceded a point of terrain of the truth. He never compromised or bowed before disseminators and defenders of lies. He even smiled at them as such. We have his books, which still speak, his writings, which still cry out, his pastoral letters, each of which is a thunderclap that brings terror to the enemy. All of these prove his strength in defending the integrity of the faith and that he was the bishop that was needed by the Church in these times.

Do you wish for even stronger, more conclusive proof of the strength of the Most Reverend Schumacher in defending the integrity of the faith, a strength that the Church needs in these times in its bishops? I give it to you with pleasure, because it is proof at the same time of the great heavenly reward that we will have according to Jesus Christ's promise in the gospel. Oh enviable proof! What is it? It is the rabid hate that the enemies of Jesus

Christ had for him, the thousands of insults that they leveled against him.

Do you wish for another piece of evidence for this? The one that has the greatest worth and is the seal of all proof is *his banishment for this motive.*

But what have I just said? No, it is not the greatest proof, because the enemies of Jesus Christ gave him the honor of martyrdom. A leader of the liberals gave the order to take him prisoner. A divine influence stopped the man from daring to carry out the order, and he retreated. Agents of the lodges intended to kill the bishop, which is found in sworn declarations according to one of the individuals spoken to, the one with the mission to kill him. After the bishop had already fled Portoviejo, one night the liberals surrounded the house where he was lodged and yelled that they were going to knife him, and he himself asked: "Why haven't you knifed me already? How was I able to free myself from your hands? God intervened in a most obvious way. Yes, it is necessary to confess that for the glory of God."

That is how the deceased spoke. Listen to him again, and you will see that he was ready to give his life for the faith. He said, "When I went there to Calceta and found myself threatened with shouts of death from liberals, a young man with an excellent heart but completely filled with liberal theories visited me. He said to me, 'Father bishop, get rid of these ideas and accept ours, and then no one will kill you.' I answered him, 'God forbid! I cannot stop demanding the people of Manabis to obey the Church. If Our Lord Jesus Christ had followed the counsel that you give me, if he had embraced the ideas of the Jews, especially those of the Pharisees, he would not have been crucified.'"

Could the Most Reverend Schumacher have said more clearly that he was ready to give his life in defense of the faith? And who does not see in this response, given in moments when the horrible cries of "Die!" sounded against him, a strength that is worthy of the highest praise, and a kind of bishop who was needed by the Church in these times?

An enemy who, on the one hand, does not do any damage, and on the other hand, tries to make arrangements or compromises, is not feared by anyone. An enemy who hurts, kills, resists, and does not cede is feared. The enemies of the faith feared and hated the Most Reverend Schumacher because he caused them painful wounds and did not retreat from the fight nor capitulate. This resulted in slander, insults, yelling, death threats, banishment, and ceaseless repetition, in every tone, "We do not want you to return!" Much more could be said about all of this than what I or the most eloquent orator are capable of saying as homage to the strength of the Most Reverend Schumacher in defending the Catholic faith.

The Most Reverend did not ever return from his banishment. In that banishment, in the silent retreat of Samaniego, his soul was increasingly purified, his crown was enriched, and his eternal happiness grew in proportion to the merits that he acquired. He was ready for the granary of God, as the Bible expression puts it, and he lacked only one more step: death!

The Most Reverend Schumacher would not die in old age from the burden of suffering and ruin of sickness. *He died from his love for the other.* Typhoid fever passed its grim wagon through Samaniego, leaving houses in mourning, families in grief, and hearts in anguish. As a loving doctor for these locals, he could not leave them comfortless in those bleak days. Visiting the houses, he consoled people, taught them how to suffer, and preached of heaven. From this region he ascended to happiness. He was struck by the contagious fever when visiting the sick, and died, according to the priests who were present at his death.

Would you like to hear now of the edifying details of the few days of his illness and his last moments? Oh, how eagerly I will tell you what they told me! I am certain that you cannot hear certain things without being moved. But I cannot tell them without taxing the time too much. I came across these details after I had already written, and had almost had printed, what I have told you so far, and had not accounted for these things in calculating the time that is normally used for this type of tribute. I cannot, however, resist the desire to inform you of these details. Listen to how they make my case.

Although the Most Reverend Schumacher still retained his faculties, by July 14 he could no longer speak. Do you know what was the sole thing that he spoke and that those who surrounded his sickbed heard? It was this: I BELIEVE.

He died on the 15th at 10 p.m., the eve of the festival of Our Lady of Carmel, whose devotion he had fervently propagated in the last years.

Samaniego's locals stood just outside the house, and when they were told that he had died, some said, "Our father the bishop has died." Others said, "What shall become of us and of our villages?" Still others cried. Weeping and sobbing were heard at the funeral over the prayers.

There is no doubt that the soul of the Most Reverend Schumacher was filled with the ineffable joy of the words of Jesus, contained in the gospels, that promise comfort to those who suffer for his cause and his name: "Blessed shall you be when men shall hate you, and when they shall separate you, and shall reproach you, and cast out your name as evil, for the Son of man's sake. Be glad in that day and rejoice; for behold, your reward is great in heaven."[2]

I ask your attention for a little while longer to end this.

2   Luke 6:22–23.

Teachings of the deceased that still speak to us

Until his last moment, the Most Reverend Schumacher died building his great virtue and confessing the faith that he defended. Do not forget that his last words were I BELIEVE. This is the valiant cry of the true sons of the Church. I BELIEVE is what all of its heroes had said when they died.

The brave prelate of Portoviejo died a precious death. He is lamented, loved, and blessed by all the good children of the Church, and was made into the object of hate and persecution by the enemies of Jesus Christ. This persecution is the seal of true faith. We are not worthy of the name of "Catholic" if, like Jesus Christ, we are not the target of hatred and persecution by the wicked.

The great bishop died as a victim of charity. The enemies of Jesus Christ made him a victim of the faith in a thousand ways. How much glory, the Most Reverend Peter Schumacher! Such an admirable bishop! Such a valiant defender and confessor of the faith! He is a faithful and beautiful echo of the *non licet* of John the Baptist and of the *non possumus* of the popes! Like that, like that you had to die, with all this glory. Like that you had to die, with this reputation of goodness, charity, and saintliness, for the confusion of your enemies.

You are just, Lord, and just are your judgments! For this you wanted the world to see in the glorification of your servant that those who had attributed to him the worst crimes had lied in a vile and shameless way. Who would not eagerly serve you? Who would not suffer for your holy name with pleasure?

Defunctus adhuc loquitur. The deceased still speaks. He refutes his slanderers with his admirable virtues, his works that were beneficial to the people, his doctrines, and his precious death.

Defunctus adhuc loquitur. The deceased still speaks. He condemns modern impiety, modern errors, and all the freedoms of damnation included under the name *liberalism.*

Defunctus adhuc loquitur. The deceased still speaks. He denounces to the world the great sin of these tolerant Catholics who, in his words, "want to be on good terms with the enemies of the religion without clashing with those who defend it, who with hat in hand greets both sides."

Defunctus adhuc loquitur. The deceased still speaks. He anathematizes with his perseverance those who pass to the side of the enemy or get tired during the fight and abandon the battlefield.

Defunctus adhuc loquitur. The deceased still speaks. He encourages the good not to fear persecution from defending the truth, and to go up to Calvary if necessary and die like the heroes, martyrs, and confessors of the faith.

Defunctus adhuc loquitur. The deceased still speaks. He appears to do these things in a prophetic tone: Listen.

On July 16, the precious remains of the Most Reverend Schumacher were exposed in the church of Samaniego, and on this very day the city of Guayaquil, where he had been so injured, caught fire. On the occasion of this fire, a newspaper in Quito asked the following: "Will it be possible to find those responsible for these dreadful crimes?" The deceased, who still speaks, answers this question stating that those responsible are those who were decatholicized by the liberal press of Guayaquil. When he was still in Portoviejo, he said in his ecclesiastical newspaper to Guayaquil's residents that "someday those who have been decatholocized by the liberal press will burn down its houses." Since then, the fire of 1896 occurred. In that year he declared in a writing: "I repeat and say that if the people do not return to the fear of God and belief in hell, the people of Guayaquil can rebuild their houses and stores all they want. The people will return to burn them down." What do you say of these prophecies?

Defunctus adhuc loquitur. The deceased still speaks. He speaks to you. Hear him, because after this I will not let him speak again for now. "To the residents of this welcoming city of Pasto, who gave me so much evidence of their affection and acceptance, to the generous people, and to the kind-hearted priests, I cannot repay them better than with a burning prayer to offer for them to the Lord. This prayer of my heart is that your country be free always from the calamities of civil war. I pray to God that Catholic Colombia, in the shadow of peace and guided by the healing teachings that emanate from the gospel, develop its means of national prosperity every day, that the motives of disagreement between its sons disappear, that the blind power of arms does not decide anything, and that this republic remain a firm and perpetual bulwark of Catholicism and Christian civilization against the advances of impiety."

May the Lord hear your prayer, endearing pastor, with your beautiful and sublime soul and beautiful heart!

Holy God! Hear the prayer of he who suffered so much for the glory of your name. If he needs our prayers, hear all that we say from the depths of our souls.

Requiem aeternam dona ei, Domine.
Requiescat in pace. Amen.

The Last Will of Monsignor Moreno

JESUS AND MARY LIVE!

In the name of the holy and indivisible Trinity, Father, Son, and Holy Spirit. Amen.

I, FATHER EZEQUIEL MORENO Y DÍAZ, of the Order of the Hermits of St. Augustine, bishop of Pasto on this date, believe and confess all the things that our holy mother the Catholic Church has declared as revealed by God, including both those made in solemn judgment and those in its ordinary and universal magisterium.

I believe and confess all of the apostolic and ecclesiastical traditions, Holy Scripture in the sense recognized by the holy Catholic Church, and all and each of the things that the general Councils, particularly from the Councils of Trent and Vatican, defined and declared, and especially the supreme and infallible magisterium of the Roman Pontiff, in whom I recognize as the Vicar of Jesus Christ on earth and the pastor and doctor of the entire Catholic Church.

I condemn all of the errors that are condemned, whether by the general Councils, especially the Vatican Council, or by the Roman Pontiffs, and especially those included under the name of liberalism, and all those listed in the *Syllabus*.

I have not made a testament because I am a religious and own nothing. I will nevertheless make a few explanations in order to provide clarity for those who must make arrangements after my death. This clarity will result from the two following principles, generally admitted by all the theologians and canonists:

1. What a member of an order acquires belongs to his religious house or order.
2. What he acquires after he is elevated to the episcopacy belongs to his cathedral parish.

According to these principles, I declare:

Everything that I point out in paragraph II until number 11 was given to me before my episcopal office and because I was going to be a bishop....

I have two poor younger sisters. I did not support them during my episcopacy in Pasto because I had no means to do so. I gave them money for all their necessities from here, except what I spent on food and attire, and then I brought enough clothes from Bogotá.

In the document that is added to this one, I have made a few notes that can be added to my *Instruction* on the conduct of liberals that can be observed.

I once again confess that liberalism is a sin, the fatal enemy of the Church and of the reign of Jesus Christ. It is the ruin of peoples and nations. Wanting to teach this, even after my death, I desire that in the hall in which my remains are exposed, and even in the church during the funeral rite, a large sign be placed so that everyone can see and on which is written: "Liberalism is a sin."

I desire and request that I be interred in my holy religious habit, as a son of my great father St. Augustine, and that I be buried in the earth of the Sacrament Chapel of the Cathedral. For the rest, all that the Church commands in the Roman Pontifical for the interment of a bishop should be followed. I oppose nothing about this solemnity because it is ordained by the Church.

I ask for forgiveness for my faults in the carrying out of my pastoral charge: first, from God our Lord; second, from my beloved clergy; third, from all the believers of the diocese, and from all those whom I have offended in the course of my life or have harmed in some way, either by something I have done or left undone. I ask everyone to pray to God for my poor soul.

I conclude by stating that under the sepulcher I feel great pain in seeing the attempt to de-catholicize Pasto . . . I have warned about this evil, and have even suffered for this warning. I do not repent of having made it. If I have to repent of something here, it is for not warning enough. The faith is lost more and more. Liberalism has achieved the unspeakable. . . .

> I signed for all of the above in
> Pasto on October 6, 1905.
> ✝ Fr. Ezequiel
> Bishop of Pasto

Solemn Rite of Beatification of Five Servants of God[1]

HOMILY OF HIS HOLINESS PAUL VI

ALL SAINTS' DAY, NOVEMBER 1, 1975

I. THE CHURCH ONCE AGAIN REJOICES over five of her heroic sons. In this Holy Year, the distinguishing features of sanctity of the Church shine in a particular way: "The universal call to holiness," brought to light by the Second Vatican Council (*Lumen Gentium*, 39–42) for all the groups of the Church—bishops, priests, religious, laity in all conditions and states—are marvelously confirmed in these strong, humble, and, until now, unknown figures. They are nevertheless rich in examples of miracles and admirable memories that provide suitable, familiar, and achievable models for us. Their pledges of hard-working dedication to God and to their brothers shake us up. Yet again, God is glorified in these Blessed. The Church does not cease to produce sons who spread his Name through their concrete and persuasive testimony of theological virtue. The Church gives testimony to the

---

1   This section is an excerpt of Pope Paul VI's homily which pertains to the then beatified Ezequiel Moreno.

world of its deepest and most vital secrets regarding the sanctifying power that fills everything and comes from the heart itself of the One and Triune God. But the human race is also ennobled and embellished because the Church continues to produce from its womb champions of humanity who are filled with faithfulness to the grace of the Lord. These champions say to us that, in spite of everything, goodness exists, goodness keeps working, and goodness spreads, even quietly. In the end, its beneficial influence overcomes the deafening but sterile and depressing noise of evil.

II. OUR FIVE PERSONALITIES HONOR THE modern era. What they have in common is the consecration of their souls to God through the priesthood and religious life. Their lives were so rich that each would require a separate discussion.

1. The first of our newly-Blessed is Ezequiel Moreno, a friar and bishop, and one more glory for Catholic Spain. Born in Alfaro (Logroño) in 1848, he later entered the family of the Augustine Recollects. His zeal went beyond the frontiers of his country, first in the Philippines, where he was ordained to the priesthood and developed his apostolate in Manila, the Palawan islands, and Imus. Afterwards, he served at the Novitiate College in Monteagudo (Navarra), and then as Apostolic Vicar of Casanare, Colombia, and Bishop of Pasto, also in Colombia. His indefatigable zeal never let up when he preached the Word of God, administered the sacrament of reconciliation, cared for the sick day and night, and firmly defended his flock from the errors of the day. Yet he also expressed great love and gentleness for those who had been misguided.

His love for the Cross, such as contained in his reflections during his painful sickness that led to his death in

1906, deserves special mention. He is a living example of sanctity for bishops, whose "perfect duty of pastoral charity is exercised in every form of episcopal care and service, prayer, sacrifice and preaching. By this same sacramental grace, they are given the courage necessary to lay down their lives for their sheep, and the ability of promoting greater holiness in the Church by their daily example, having become a pattern for their flock" (*Lumen Gentium*, 41).

✦ ✦ ✦

III. THE MESSAGE THAT THE NEW Blessed spread to us is shared by all those who take the gospel seriously: to love God "with thy whole heart, and with thy whole soul, and with thy whole mind" (Matt. 22:37), and to love our neighbor as ourselves. This is the royal road to sanctity, outside of which there is nothing worthy of the Kingdom of God. The Blessed Moreno, Bertoni, Grossi, Michelotti, and Droste truly loved the Lord and their brothers in this way. Despite differences in the expressions of their piety, as in their lives, we find the common features of Christian sanctity. But together they also tell us something particular, which is care for the young, the love of the Cross and suffering, and love for the Blessed Virgin.

1. Concern for the young: In the variety of their initiatives and works, these Blessed all perceived, with a striking clear-sightedness, the need to listen to the young out of the certainty that these young people are the future of the Church and society. This is a serious warning for our time and a cause for reflection for bishops, priests, and religious. This concern invites us to devote more and better energy to the marvelous energy of the young, who are capable of ensuring the vitality of the Christian community, the health of families, the continuity of vocations, and generous engagement for a better future.

2. Our new Beati still speak to us about the love of the Cross, for all of them have suffered and desired to suffer even to the heights of heroism. And this heroism has been all the greater in that it has been concealed in detachment, poverty, difficulties, misunderstandings, sickness, and hidden lives. This is just like a grain that falls to the earth and dies in order to produce much fruit (Cfr. John 12:24). And with this same dedication they have loved those who have been marked by the Cross more than anyone else: the poor and the sick. The Blessed have discovered in the poor and the sick the disfigured countenance of Christ. This is indeed a relevant lesson today, when the wave of hedonism, the search for comfort at any cost, and deafness to the needs of others are threatening to make people forget that the greater part of humanity suffers from material and spiritual ills. The civilization of a people is measured by its sensitivity in the face of suffering and its capacity to relieve it!

3. The newly-Blessed still speak to us about their love for the Blessed Virgin Mary, who constantly inspired their apostolates and accompanied them with her illuminating example. As the Mother of God and Mother of the Church, Mary "cooperates with a maternal love" for the "birth and education" of the faithful (*Lumen Gentium*, 63). Therefore, she is present in the hidden lives of the saints in a special way. We would therefore like to conclude that our thoughts are directed to her. She is the Queen of all the saints whom we honor today. She is the glory of paradise in the virginal beauty of her transfigured body, which is the temple of the incarnate Word of God. She is also the Queen of all the saints in the splendor of her soul's incomparable holiness, which is full of grace.

Today, in raising our reverential thoughts towards the Blessed Virgin, and guided by the example of our new Blessed, we cannot fail to highlight a happy coincidence:

It was precisely twenty years ago, on this same day and at this same place, that our predecessor Pius XII solemnly proclaimed the Assumption of Mary to heaven, in an explosion of joy for the Church: "all generations shall call me blessed" (Luke 1:48). To her we entrust our lives, the various ups and downs of the present world, and the entire Church. We pray that Mary will help and guide us, and find us willing and meek, like the new Blessed. We consecrate ourselves, with her and with them, like her and like them, to the glory of the Father, the Son, and the Holy Spirit.

Apostolic Voyage to Santo Domingo

HOLY MASS ON THE CENTENARY
OF THE EVANGELIZATION OF
THE BLESSED EZEQUIEL MORENO
Y DÍAZ AND HIS CANONIZATION

HOMILY OF HIS HOLINESS
JOHN PAUL II
Faro a Colón, Santo Domingo
Sunday, October 11, 1992

Arise, be enlightened, O Jerusalem:
for thy light is come. (Isa. 60:1)

1. THE COMMEMORATION OF THE FIFTH
centennial of the beginning of the evangelization of the
New World is a great day for the Church.

As successor of the Apostle Peter, I have the joy to
celebrate this Eucharist together with my brother bishops
of all of Latin America, along with other invited bishops,
in this blessed land that, five hundred years ago, received
Christ, light of the nations, and was marked with the
sign of the Cross that brings salvation.

From Santo Domingo, I desire to join with all of
America's beloved sons my affectionate greeting with the
words of the Apostle Paul: "Grace be to you, and peace
from God the Father, and from our Lord Jesus Christ"
(Gal. 1:3). To commemorate October 12, 1492, which

is one of the most important dates in human history, I direct my affections and thoughts to each and every individual church on the American continent. Despite the distance, I extend my voice to all of you along with my close presence.

2. A VOICE THAT EMBRACES IN THE name of the Lord the Churches in the Southern Cone: Chile and Argentina, Uruguay and Paraguay.

A voice of brotherly love in Christ for the Church in Brazil, for the Churches in the Andean countries: Bolivia and Peru, Ecuador and Colombia.

A voice of affectionate communion in the faith with the Church in Venezuela, Surinam, the Antilles, the Dominican Republic and Haiti, in Cuba, Jamaica, and Puerto Rico.

A voice of peace in the Lord for the Church of Central America and Panama, Mexico and North America.

Together with the fraternal embrace of my brothers in the Episcopate, I desire to convey my cordial and respectful greeting to the President of the Republic and the other authorities who accompany us.

3. THE WORDS OF ISAIAH, PROCLAIMED in the first reading, "Arise, be enlightened, O Jerusalem: for thy light is come" (Isa. 60:1), present us with the glory of the new Jerusalem. From the distance of centuries, the prophet announces He whom he sees as the Light of the world. From Jerusalem comes the dawn that will shine in the fullness of the Divine mystery designed from all eternity. Its brilliance will reach all the nations of the earth.

Today in Santo Domingo, gathered around the altar in thanksgiving to God, we celebrate the arrival of the light that illuminated the way of the people with the light of life and hope. Five hundred years ago, these people were

brought to the Christian faith. With the force of the Holy
Spirit, the redeeming work of Christ was made present
with the great number of missionaries who, prompted
by the Lord's mandate to "preach the gospel to every
creature" (Mark 16:15), crossed the ocean to announce
the message of salvation to their brothers. Together with
my brother bishops of America, I give thanks to the
Holy Trinity because "All the ends of the earth have seen
the salvation of our God" (Psalm 97:3).[1] The prophet's
words became truth and life on this continent of hope.
For this, with unrestrained joy, we can today proclaim
once again: America, "Arise, be enlightened, O Jerusalem:
for thy light is come, and the glory of the Lord is risen
upon thee" (Isa. 60:1).

4. AND WHAT COULD BE A GREATER
honor for America than presenting *testimonies of sanctity* that throughout these five centuries have brought the
message of Jesus Christ to life in the New World? An
admirable number of saints and blessed adorns almost all
of the Americas. Their lives represent the most mature
fruits of evangelization and are the models and inspiration
for new evangelists.

This holy setting hosts the present canonization of
Blessed Ezequiel Moreno. In his life and apostolic work,
he admirably brings together the central elements of the
events that we celebrate today. In the summary of his holy
life, as well as in the heavenly merits and graces that the
Lord desired to adorn him with—which we have heard
only a few moments ago while officially requesting his
canonization—Spain, the Philippines, and Latin America
appear as the places in which the tireless missionary work
of this distinguished son of the Order of the Augustine

---

1   The original reference in both the Italian and Spanish versions
indicate Ps. 98:3. The Douay-Rheims is 97:3.

Recollects developed. As bishop of Pasto, Colombia, he felt particularly driven by the apostolic zeal that, as we heard in the second reading of this liturgical celebration, led St. Paul to proclaim, "How then shall they call on him, in whom they have not believed? Or how shall they believe him, of whom they have not heard? And how shall they hear, without a preacher?" (Rom. 10:14).

5. ABOVE ALL, THIS NEW SAINT PRESents us with a *model of an evangelist*, whose unstoppable desire to announce Christ guided every step of his life. In Casanare, Arauca, Pasto, Santafé de Bogotá, and so many other places, he devoted himself unreservedly to preaching, the sacrament of reconciliation, catechesis, and assistance to the sick. His unshakable faith in God, sustained at every moment by an intense interior life, was the great strength that supported him in his dedication to the service to everyone, in particular to the poorest and most abandoned. As a profoundly spiritual and vigilant pastor, he gave life to various religious associations, and wherever he could not go in person, he made his presence felt through publications, newspapers, and personal letters.

With his life and evangelical work, St. Ezequiel Moreno is a model for pastors, especially in Latin America. Under the guidance of the Holy Spirit, these pastors seek to respond with new energy, methods, and expressions for the great challenges that the Church in Latin America faces. This Church, called to Christianity's most precious gift, which is holiness, must therefore ceaselessly proclaim, "Jesus Christ, yesterday, and today" (Heb. 13:8). The Lord Jesus, who was announced for the first time to the peoples of this continent five hundred years ago, brings us salvation, because only He has the words of eternal life (cf. John 6:69). "For God so loved

the world, as to give his only begotten Son; that whosoever believeth in him, may not perish, but may have
life everlasting" (John 3:16). This is the God who loves
man to the point that he gives his life for him. This is
the incarnated God who dies and is resurrected. He is
the God of Love!

Today, together with the whole Church, we raise our
thanksgiving for these five hundred years of evangelization. In truth, the words of the prophet Isaiah that we
heard have been fulfilled: "Thy heart shall wonder and be
enlarged, when the multitude of the sea shall be converted
to thee" (Isa. 60:5). This is the wealth of faith, hope,
and love. This is "the strength of the Gentiles" (Ibid):
their worth, knowledge, and culture. Throughout history,
the Church has known tests and divisions, and has felt
enriched by He who is the Lord of history.

ABOUT THE TRANSLATOR

BRIAN WELTER teaches advanced high school reading and writing. He is interested in French literature, medieval history and aesthetics. He has a BA in history and degrees in theology, including the DTh. He also has a graduate diploma in teaching English. In addition to French, he reads Italian, German, and Latin. He has translated the following two French works into English: *Salazar and His Work: Essays on Political Philosophy* by Marcel de Corte, Pierre Gaxotte, and Gustave Thibon (Arouca Press, 2021) and *Immortal Latin* by Marie-Madeleine Martin (Arouca Press, 2021).